VICTORIAN QUILTING

VICTORIAN QUILTING

THE VANESSA-ANN COLLECTION

BALLANTINE BOOKS ∾ NEW YORK

Produced for Ballantine Books
by
THE VANESSA-ANN COLLECTION

DESIGNERS

Jo Packham
Debbie Thurgood
Susan Whitelock

STAFF

Jo Packham and Terrece Woodruff, owners

Ana Ayala, Gloria Baur, Trice Boerens, Vicki
Burke, Lisa Dayton, Tim Fairholm, Susan
Jorgensen, Margaret Marti, Barbara Milburn, Lisa
Miles, Lynda Morrison, Pam Randall, Leslie
Rodak, Reva Smith, Julie Truman, Nancy Whitley

The home of Debra and David Johnson, Salt Lake
City, Utah, was used for the photography in this
book. The Vanessa-Ann Collection appreciates
their trust and cooperation.

Photography by Mikel Covey

Chapelle Designers
P.O. Box 9252 Newgate Station
Ogden, Utah 84403

© 1990 by Chapelle Designers

Library of Congress Catalog Number: 89-92600
ISBN: 0-345-36404-X
Manufactured in the United States of America
First Edition: November 1990

10 9 8 7 6 5 4 3 2 1

Judy,
   Here's to you, to happiness
and to us—we just might
make it after all!
                    Love,
                    Jo

What are Victorian quilts made of?

Snips of lace,
buttons and pearls,
and oodles of beads and bows

Delicate flowers,
fancy fans,
and ribbons dancing in rows.

That's what Victorian quilts are made of.

In *Victorian Quilting* we have recaptured the rich legacy of elegance and style associated with a by-gone era. Opulent, and even extravagant at times, these quilts are a treasury of intricate needle art at its finest. Your creations will evoke the same enduring charm as the age they represent, and we know you will spend some of your most treasured moments fashioning your own album of memories in fabric. Enjoy!

CONTENTS

MORNING GLORY

"Every flower about a house certifies to the refinement of somebody. Every vine climbing and blossoming tells of love and joy."

Robert G. Ingersoll

Fabrics needed:

Light green: 3 1/2" yards

Muslin: 5 yards

Batting:

Cut sizes:

Twenty-two 5 1/2" x 5 1/2" pieces
Fifteen 5 1/2" x 10" pieces
Two 10 1/2" x 66" border strips
Two 10 1/2" x 59" border strips
8 yards of 3"-wide bias strips

Twenty 5 1/2" x 5 1/2" pieces
Twelve 7 1/2" x 7 1/2" pieces for embroidery
Twelve 7 1/2" x 11 1/2" pieces for embroidery
Two 35 1/2" x 81" pieces for backing

One 66" x 79" pieces

Also needed:

Cream thread for quilting
Embroidery threads (see page 9)

Finished size: 66" x 79"

1. **Embroider.** Transfer embroidery patterns, placing single flower motifs on 7 1/2" x 7 1/2" muslin pieces and double flower motifs on 7 1/2" x 11 1/2" muslin pieces. Embroider according to patterns (see General Instructions for embroidery techniques). Trim 7 1/2" x 7 1/2" pieces to 5 1/2" x 5 1/2" and 7 1/2" x 11 1/2" pieces to 5 1/2" x 10", centering designs.

2. **Construct quilt top.** Row 1: Stitch together four 5 1/2" x 5 1/2" muslin pieces, three 5 1/2" x 5 1/2" green pieces, and two single flower embroidered pieces, positioning flower toward center of quilt (see Schematic). Repeat for Row 9.

   Row 2: Stitch together three 5 1/2" x 5 1/2" muslin pieces, four 5 1/2" x 5 1/2" green pieces, and two single flower embroidered pieces (see Schematic). Repeat for Rows 4, 6 and 8.

   Row 3: Stitch together five 5 1/2" x 10" green pieces and four double flower embroi-dered pieces (see Schematic). Repeat for Rows 5 and 7.

   Stitch rows together according to Schematic.

3. **Add border.** Stitch one 10 1/2" x 79 1/2" border strip to each side edge of quilt. Stitch one 10 1/2" x 66" border strip to top and bottom of quilt.

4. **Mark quilting lines.** In each green rectangle, center eight square patterns and mark quilting lines. In each empty

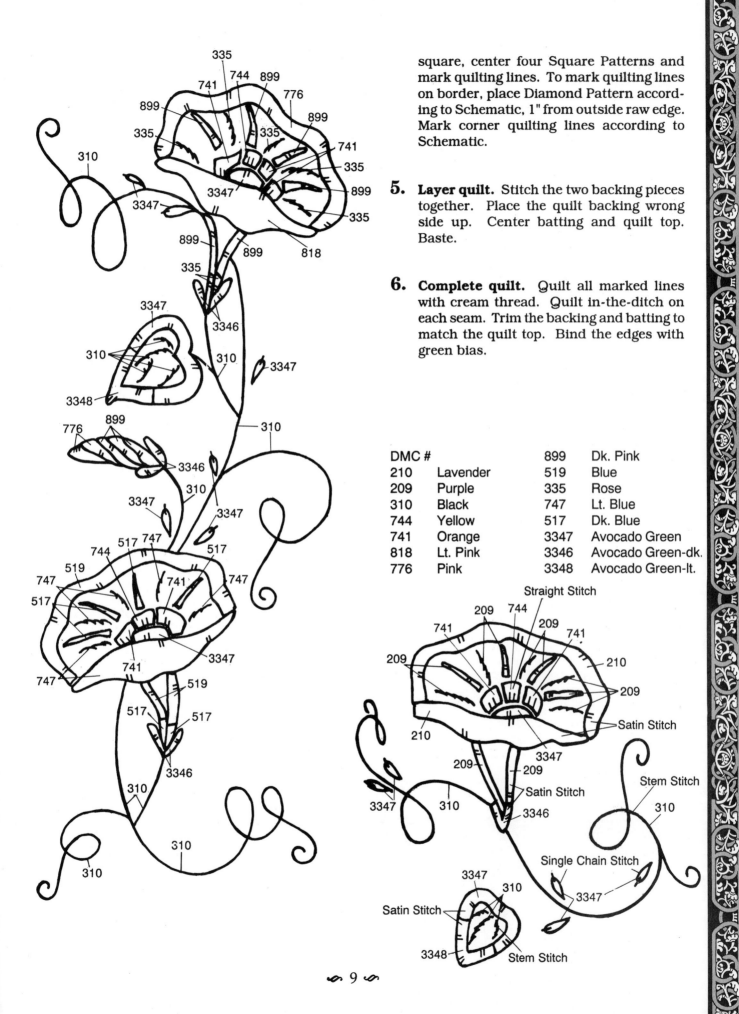

square, center four Square Patterns and mark quilting lines. To mark quilting lines on border, place Diamond Pattern according to Schematic, 1" from outside raw edge. Mark corner quilting lines according to Schematic.

5. Layer quilt. Stitch the two backing pieces together. Place the quilt backing wrong side up. Center batting and quilt top. Baste.

6. Complete quilt. Quilt all marked lines with cream thread. Quilt in-the-ditch on each seam. Trim the backing and batting to match the quilt top. Bind the edges with green bias.

DMC #			
210	Lavender	899	Dk. Pink
209	Purple	519	Blue
310	Black	335	Rose
744	Yellow	747	Lt. Blue
741	Orange	517	Dk. Blue
818	Lt. Pink	3347	Avocado Green
776	Pink	3346	Avocado Green-dk.
		3348	Avocado Green-lt.

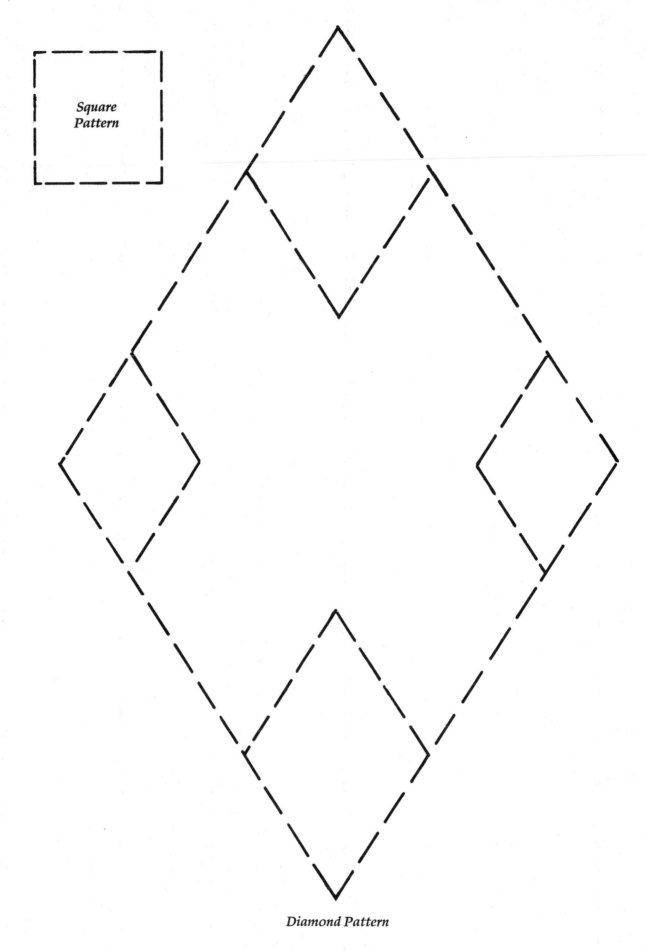

Square
Pattern

Diamond Pattern

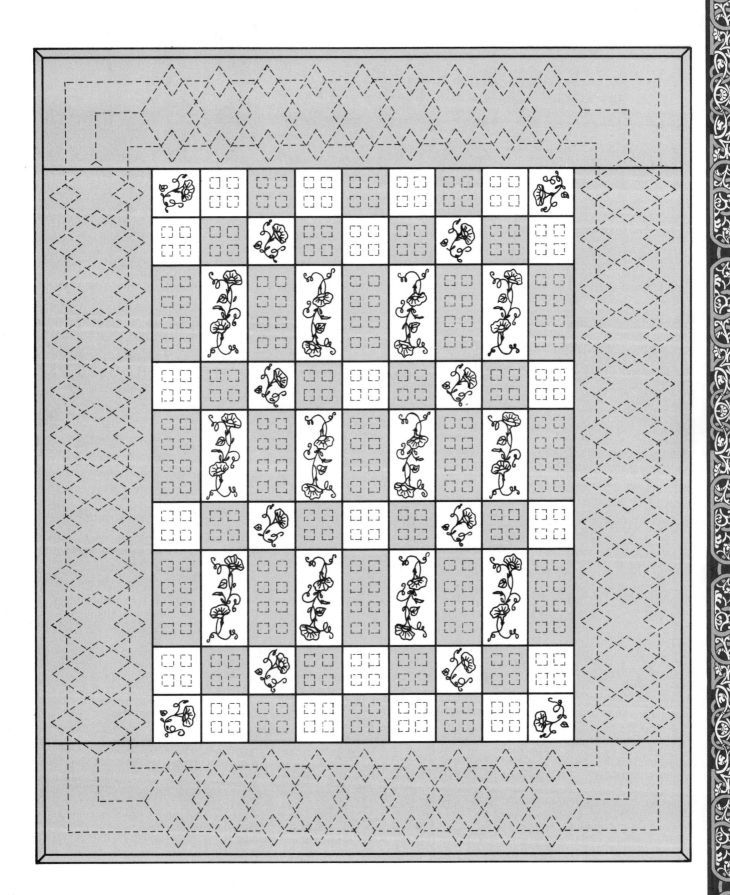

Schematic

PATCHWORK PAIR

We'll talk of sunshine and of song,
And summer days when we were young
Sweet childish days that were as long
As twenty days are now.

William Wordsworth

QUILT:

Finished size: 11" x 13½"

Fabrics needed:	Cut sizes:
Pink: ¼ yard	Twelve 2½" x 2½" pieces Sixteen 1" x 2½" sashing pieces Five 1" x 8½" sashing pieces
Three assorted prints: scraps	Six of Template A* from Print 1 Six of Template A* from Print 2 Twelve of Template D* from Print 3
Brown: ⅛ yard	Twelve of Template B* Two 1" x 9" border strips Two 1" x 11" border strips
Green/black print: ½ yard	Twelve of Template C* One 15" x 18" backing piece
Flannel: scrap	One 11" X 13½" piece

Also needed:

White thread
Assorted beads, small buttons, laces and trims

*See Step 1 before cutting

PILLOW:

Finished size: 10½" X 10½"

Fabrics needed:	Cut sizes:
Green/lavender print: scrap	One of Template E*
Dark red: scrap	One of Template F*
Pink: scrap	One 10½" x 10½" piece
Faded red: scrap	One of Template G*
Green/black print: ½ yard	One of Template H* One 10½" x 10½" backing piece 45" of 1¼"-wide bias for corded piping
Flannel: scrap	One 10½" x 10½" piece

Also needed:

8" of ½"-wide lace
Four ¼"-wide blue buttons
6" of ⅝"-wide mauve satin ribbon
8" of ¾"-wide beaded trim
Pink thread for quilting
1½"-wide beaded applique
Five pink beads
Four dozen iridescent bugle beads
Two decorated hat pins; see Step 6
1¼ yards of medium cording
One 12" x 12" pillow form

QUILT:

1. Prepare fabric. Make templates from patterns. Trace each template onto $2\frac{1}{2}$" x $2\frac{1}{2}$" pink pieces to make placement guide. Then, adding $\frac{1}{4}$" seam allowances, use Templates A, B, C and D to cut fabric pieces.

2. Prepare twelve blocks. Place one print A piece at top of block. Fold under seam allowance on lower edge; slipstitch. Repeat with prints B, C and D, folding under edge which is toward center. Repeat to make 12 blocks, adding small pieces of lace or trim, as desired, and securing them in seam allowance.

3. Piece quilt top. Arrange blocks in four rows of three each. Stitch blocks into rows with short sashing pieces between them (Diagram 1). Stitch rows together using long sashing pieces (Diagram 1). Stitch one long brown border piece to each side edge of block. Then stitch one short brown border piece to the top and bottom edges.

4. Embellish quilt. Attach trim, beads and buttons as desired; see photo.

5. Layer quilt. Place the quilt backing wrong side up. Center the flannel and quilt top. Baste.

Trim backing to $1\frac{1}{4}$" outside flannel on all edges. Fold to the front, turning under $\frac{1}{4}$" on edge, to make a 1"-wide border, mitering the corners. Slipstitch.

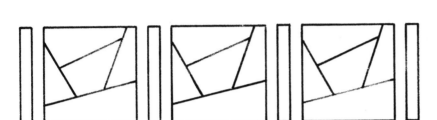

Diagram 1

Quilt Schematic

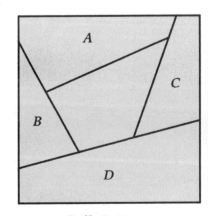

Quilt Patterns

6. Complete quilt. Mark ³/4" intervals on one edge of brown border. Then mark ³/4" intervals on opposite edge, placing second marks half-way between first. Mark zigzag pattern. Quilt on zigzag pattern with white thread.

PILLOW:

1. Prepare fabric. Enlarge the patterns on the grid to make full-size templates. Trace onto pink piece to make placement guide. Then adding ¹/4" seam allowances, use templates E, F, G and H to cut fabric pieces.

2. Applique ribbon. Place mauve ribbon across pink center section (see photo). Fold ends under and applique to pink fabric.

3. Applique pillow top. Place green print E at top of block. Fold under seam allowance on lower edge; slipstitch. Repeat with F, G and H pieces, folding under edge which is toward center.

4. Quilt pillow top. Layer pillow top over flannel. Baste. Echo quilt left triangular area of pink center section in three rows ¹/8" apart using pink thread. Echo quilt right area of pink center ¹/8" from seam lines.

5. Construct pillow top. Make 45" of corded piping. Stitch corded piping to pillow front. Stitch pillow front and back together, sewing on stitching line of corded piping and leaving an opening on one side. Clip corners. Turn. Insert pillow form. Slipstitch opening closed.

6. Embellish pillow. Attach trim, beads and buttons as desired; see photo. (The bugle beads are attached to follow a pattern in one of the print fabrics.)

To make the large decorated hat pin, cut two ³/4" x ³/4" pieces of fabric. Whipstitch the edges, inserting the head of a hat pin between the layers and a small amount of stuffing before whipstitching the fourth edge. Embellish further with looped strings of pink beads. To make the small decorated hat pin, cut one 1" piece of ⁵/8"-wide grosgrain ribbon. Fold under raw edges and fold ribbon to ¹/4" x ⁵/8". Whipstitch edges, inserting head of hat pin and a small amount of stuffing.

Pillow Patterns

Finished size: 48" x 72"

Fabrics needed: | **Cut sizes:**

Patterned and/or assorted solid colors: scraps	800 of Template A 1600 of Template B
Black taffeta: 3 1/2 yards	800 of Template A 175 of Template B 50" x 70" piece for backing
Flannel: 2 yards	51" x 75" piece

Also needed:

Black thread

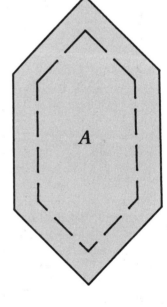

HONEYCOMB MASTERPIECE

She sews the bits together,
And, intricate or plain,
Beneath her flying fingers
Grows basket, star or chain.

Grace Noll Crowell

1. Construct quilt top. Stitch long edge of patterned or solid A to black A, stopping 1/4" from each end. Continue with all As. Then stitch A/A blocks together, alternating black blocks (Diagram 1), to make 45"-wide rows.

Set aside one row of As. Except for this row, stitch patterned or solid Bs to top edge of rows of As (Diagram 2), stopping 1/4" from each edge. (Stitching should meet seam joining As.) Then stitch rows together, alternating black blocks; see photo. Continue until quilt measures 63 3/4" long. Stitch re-maining row of As to top edge of quilt.

Stitch row of black Bs to all outside edges of quilt top. Trim edges to make straight, leaving a 1/4" seam allowance.

2. Complete quilt. Place the quilt backing wrong side up. Center and layer flannel and quilt top over backing. Baste. Trim backing 1" outside quilt top.

Fold backing double to front making a 1/2"-wide binding. Slipstitch to quilt top.

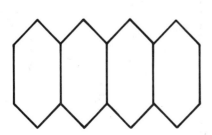

Diagram 1

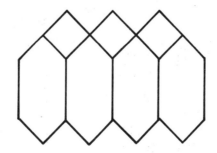

Diagram 2

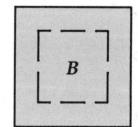

AUTUMN LEAVES

*Listen! The wind is rising,
and the air is wild with leaves,
We have had our summer evenings,
now for October eves!*

Humbert Wolfe

Finished size: 12" x 12"

$^3/8$ yard of cream heavy-weight wool felt; matching thread
2 yards of $^3/4$"-wide cinnamon silk ribbon
Six $^5/8$"-wide black buttons
Floss: Nova rayon #166
Soft-lead pencil
One medium-sized basket; see photo

1. Cut one 12" x 12" piece of felt. Trace twelve leaf patterns onto wrong side of remaining felt. Cut out.

2. Mark position for $^1/2$"-deep cuts in 12" x 12" felt piece (Diagram 1). Adjust placement for the corner cuts so that they do not meet. Trace border pattern onto wrong side of felt, aligning the scalloped edges with the edge of the felt. Cut out.

3. Mark veins on leaf. Embroider an outline stitch on each leaf.

4. Place three leaves over each corner of liner. Tack ends to liner. Also tack leaves to edge of liner. Sew two buttons over ends of three corners.

5. Thread ribbon through cuts in liner, beginning at corner without buttons and leaving a 22" tail. Allow extra fullness at each corner. Tie ribbon into bow with 4"-long loops. Trim ends. Place in basket, positioning as desired.

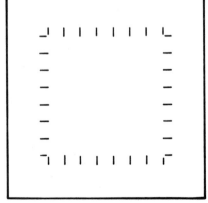

Diagram 1

POINSETTIA TABLE RUNNER

Are not flowers the stars of earth,
and are not our stars the flowers of heaven?

Anonymous

TABLE RUNNER:

2 yards of muslin fabric;
   matching thread
$3/4$ yard of khaki fabric; matching thread
$3/4$ yard of rose fabric; matching thread
2 yards of polyester fleece
Cream embroidery floss

Finished size: 18" x 72"

NAPKIN:

$1/2$ yard of muslin fabric
$1/2$ yard of khaki fabric; match-
   ing thread
Small pieces of rose fabric;
   matching thread
Small pieces of polyester fabric
Cream embroidery floss
One $1/2$"-wide button

Finished size: 15" x 15"

TABLE RUNNER:

1. Make patterns for petals of large and small poinsettias, and leaf, transferring all information. Enlarge and make pattern for end of table runner.

2. Cut two 18" x 72" pieces from muslin fabric. Cut ends according to pattern. From fleece, cut one 18" x 72" piece, cutting ends according to pattern.

3. Cut petals for two large and three small poinsettias from rose fabric. Cut sixteen leaf pieces from khaki fabric. Also from khaki fabric, cut 2"-wide bias strips, piecing as needed, to equal 5 yards for binding.

4. Trim $1/4$" seam allowance from edges of each pattern piece. Trace entire design onto ends of one muslin piece (Diagram 1). Applique design in sequence indicated in diagram.

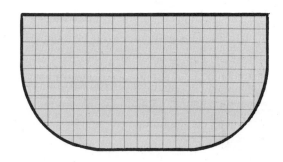

Pattern for end of Table Runner
1 square = 1"

5. Mark veins in leaves and petals. Blanket stitch each vein with one strand of cream floss. Make twelve French knots in the center of each poinsettia, using two strands of floss wrapped around the needle twice.

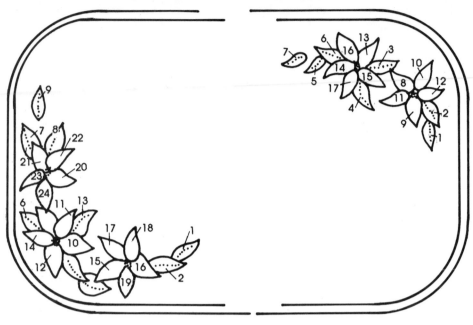

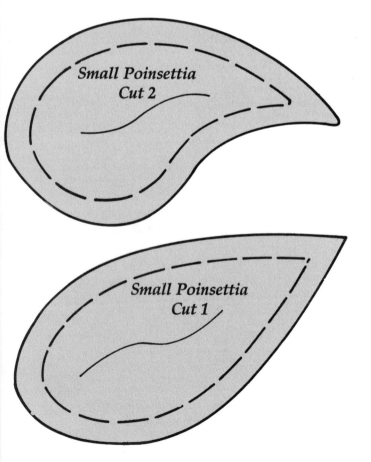

Diagram 1

6. Layer backing wrong side up, then fleece, then table runner top. Baste. Stitch binding to right side of table runner top with $^3/8"$ seam allowance. Fold binding double to back and slipstitch.

7. Quilt by hand with one strand of cream floss around each appliqued piece.

NAPKIN:

1. From muslin fabric cut one 15" x 15" piece. From rose fabric cut one set of small poinsettia petals including seam allowances. Flip patterns and cut second set of petals including seam allowances. From khaki fabric cut four leaves including seam allowances. Flip leaf pattern and cut four more leaves, including seam allowances. Also from khaki fabric cut 2"-wide bias strips, piecing as needed to equal 2 yards for binding. From fleece, cut one set of small poinsettia petals and four leaves including seam allowances. Following manufacturer's instructions, cover button with muslin fabric.

2. Stitch binding to right side of napkin with $^3/8"$ seam allowances. Fold binding double to back and slipstitch.

3. Mark veins in one set of petals and four leaves. Blanket stitch each vein with one strand of cream floss.

Small Poinsettia Cut 2

Small Poinsettia Cut 1

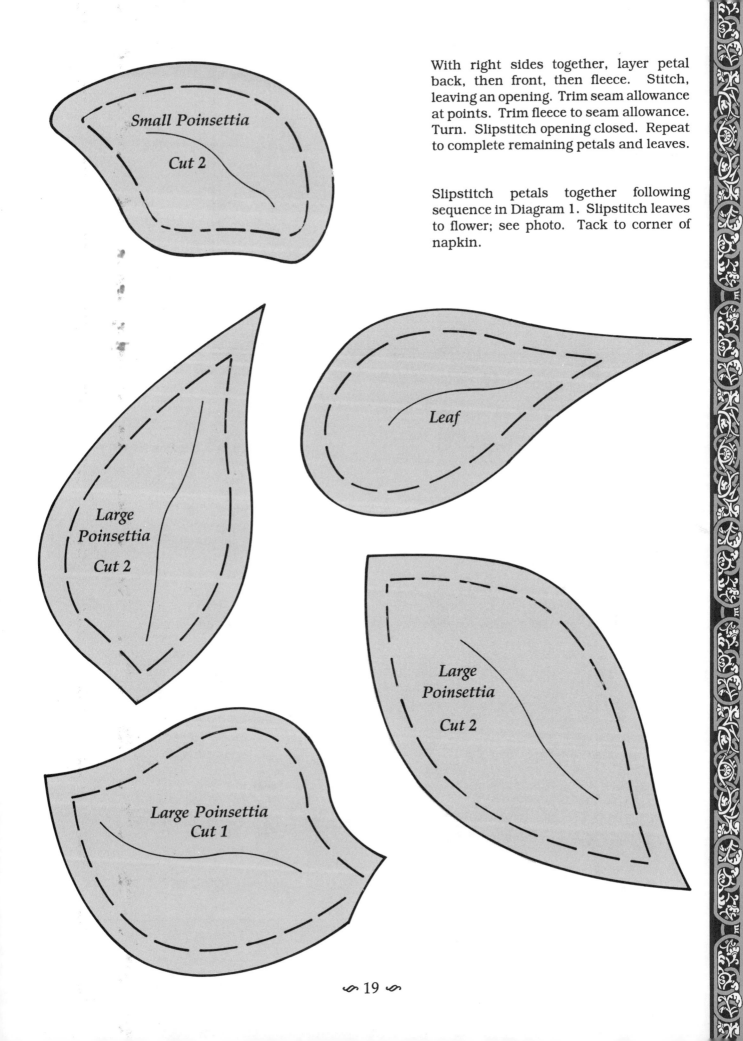

Small Poinsettia

Cut 2

With right sides together, layer petal back, then front, then fleece. Stitch, leaving an opening. Trim seam allowance at points. Trim fleece to seam allowance. Turn. Slipstitch opening closed. Repeat to complete remaining petals and leaves.

Slipstitch petals together following sequence in Diagram 1. Slipstitch leaves to flower; see photo. Tack to corner of napkin.

Large Poinsettia

Cut 2

Leaf

Large Poinsettia

Cut 2

Large Poinsettia

Cut 1

FANCY THAT!

"In the ornamentation of one's home, be it a mansion or a cottage, a regal suite of apartments or a tiny room, the clever woman takes advantage of what is pretty, popular and suitable for the purpose."

Herbert M. Ross, 1892

Finished size: 15" x 26"

Fabrics needed:	Cut sizes:
White cotton: 1 yard	One 16" x 27" piece for back Two 5$\frac{1}{2}$" x 5$\frac{1}{2}$" pieces One 7$\frac{1}{2}$" x 11$\frac{1}{2}$" piece One 1$\frac{3}{4}$" x 15$\frac{1}{2}$" piece Two 15$\frac{1}{2}$" x 2$\frac{1}{4}$" pieces One 15$\frac{1}{2}$" x 7$\frac{1}{4}$" piece Three of Template B
Decorative edge from ecru linen towel or pillow case	One 15$\frac{1}{2}$" x 2$\frac{1}{4}$" piece
Ecru linen: $\frac{1}{4}$ yard	Three of Template A Ten of Template D Two of Template E Two of Template F Two of Template G Two 4$\frac{1}{2}$" x 5" pieces One 4$\frac{1}{2}$" x 5" piece with an embroidered design for center heart
Cream linen: $\frac{1}{4}$ yard or a towel or pillowcase with hemstitching. (Hemstitching is not essential for quilt design.)	Two 1$\frac{1}{2}$" x 5$\frac{1}{2}$" pieces Three 1$\frac{1}{2}$" x 11$\frac{1}{2}$" pieces One 1$\frac{1}{2}$" x 7$\frac{1}{2}$" piece Two of Template C Five of Template H
Flannel: $\frac{1}{2}$ yard	One 16" x 27" piece

Also needed:

White and cream threads
Taupe embroidery floss
Two 2¹/₂"-square cream lace doilies
  or coasters
Jewelry for embellishment
One 3" x 4" piece of taupe crocheted
  trim for right heart
Nineteen ¹/₄"-wide pearl buttons
Ten ¹/₄"-wide dark buttons with
  shanks

Five assorted ⁵/₈"-wide antique brass
  buttons
Six ⁵/₈"-long crystal faceted beads
One 1"-long crystal faceted bead
1¹/₄ yards of ¹/₈"-wide pearl beading
¹/₂ yard of 1¹/₄"-wide cream trim
2¹/₄ yards of ready-made cream muslin
  cording
Pearl beads for embellishment as
  desired
Dressmakers' pen

1. **Piece fan blocks**. Stitch together five ecru fan pieces for upper block. Pin assembled fan to one 5¹/₂" x 5¹/₂" white piece, matching straight outside edges. Pin excess into tucks at two inside seams (Diagram 1). (Tucks will be ¹/₄" deep at outside arc.) Repeat to make lower block, making two outside seams into tucks. Applique fans. Using two strands of embroidery floss, blanket stitch to secure tucks, tapering stitches toward inside edge (Diagram 2).

2. **Piece center section**. Join fan blocks with one cream 1¹/₂" x 5¹/₂" strip. Join fan block set to white 7¹/₂" x 11¹/₂" piece, using three cream

1¹/₂" x 11¹/₂" strips (Diagram 3). Stitch together three ecru As with cream 1¹/₂" x 7¹/₂" and cream 1¹/₂" x 5¹/₂". Stitch strip to center section. Join one white 15¹/₂" x 2¹/₄" strip to top edge of center section (Diagram 3).

Diagram 2

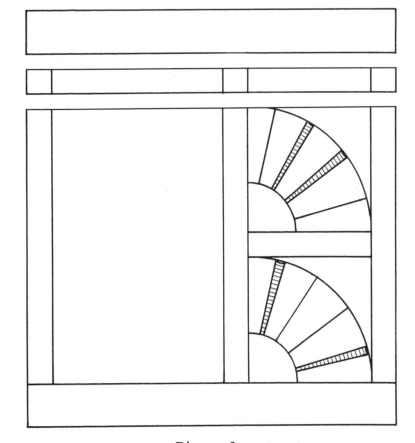

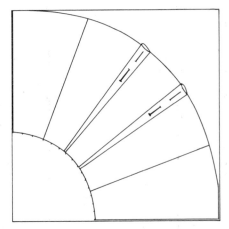

Diagram 1

Diagram 3

3. Applique tulips. Mark placement for stems (Diagram 4). Applique small leaves, then stems, large leaves, (overlapping stems) and flowers (Diagram 4). Feather-stitch leaves of left tulip using two strands of floss (see Schematic).

Pin decorative edge over $15^1/2$" x $2^1/4$" white cotton strip. Stitch to bottom edge of center section, securing both pieces in seam.

Diagram 4

4. Complete lower section. Stitch five cream Cs together. Applique three white Bs on point over the top of three Cs (Diagram 5). Applique lace doilies to remaining Cs (see Schematic).

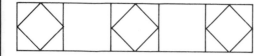

Diagram 5

Pin decorative cream trim over white $1^3/4$" x $15^1/2$" strip. Stitch to bottom edge of pieced strip, securing both pieces in seam.

Trace Bottom Pattern onto lower edge of white $15^1/2$" x

$7^1/4$" x piece. Trace hearts on this piece for placement guide. Cut $^1/4$" outside pen line. Carefully cut $^1/4$" inside each marked edge of hearts. Pin ecru $4^1/2$" x 5" pieces behind left and right hearts. Pin embroidered $4^1/2$" x 5" piece behind center heart. Clip curves. Fold seam allowances under and applique (Diagram 6). Blanket stitch edges with one strand of floss. Join lower section to strips, then join to center section, allowing decorative edge of linen to remain loose.

Diagram 6

Schematic

5. Mark quilting lines. Mark three parallel lines ¹/₂" apart on top white strip of fabric. Also mark placement for buttons (Diagram 7).

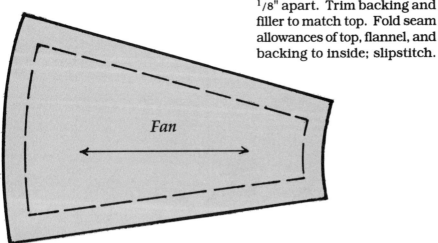

Diagram 7

6. Complete wallhanging. Cut ¹/₄" outside pen line for bottom edge. Stitch cording to right side of all edges of wallhanging with raw edges matching.

7. Layer wallhanging. Layer backing wrong side up, flannel and top. Baste. Quilt on quilting lines and close to ALL seam lines using white thread. Echo quilt the tulips in rows ¹/₈" apart. Trim backing and filler to match top. Fold seam allowances of top, flannel, and backing to inside; slipstitch.

8. Embellish quilt top. Sew ¹/₄"-wide pearl buttons on the quilting lines of the upper block (see Schematic). Sew four ¹/₄"-wide dark buttons with shanks between pearl buttons (see Schematic). Sew six ¹/₄"-wide dark buttons with shanks evenly spaced to band above hearts. Sew six crystal faceted beads to stem of right tulip. Sew pearl beading to inside circle and plain seams of each fan block. (To attach one length of beading, cut length 4" longer than amount that will show. Remove 2" of pearls at one end and secure empty thread at back of quilt; repeat at opposite end.) Sew five brass buttons and four pearl buttons to the band between the center and lower sections; see Schematic. Accent embroidered designs of center heart and cream trim with small pearl beads. Tack crochet to right heart; see photo. Embellish with jewelry as desired.

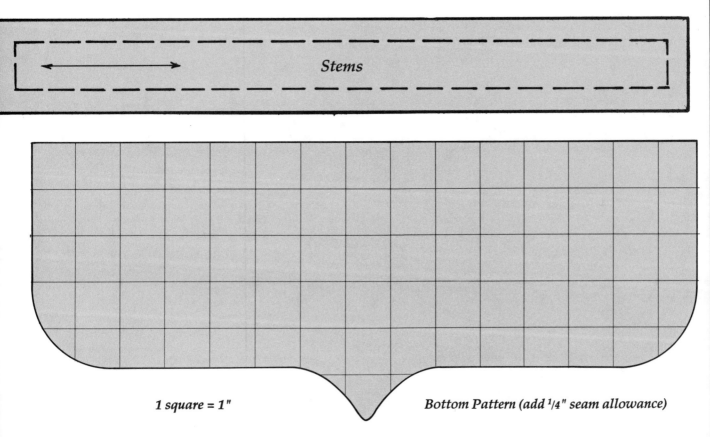

Fan

Stems

1 square = 1"

Bottom Pattern (add ¹/₄" seam allowance)

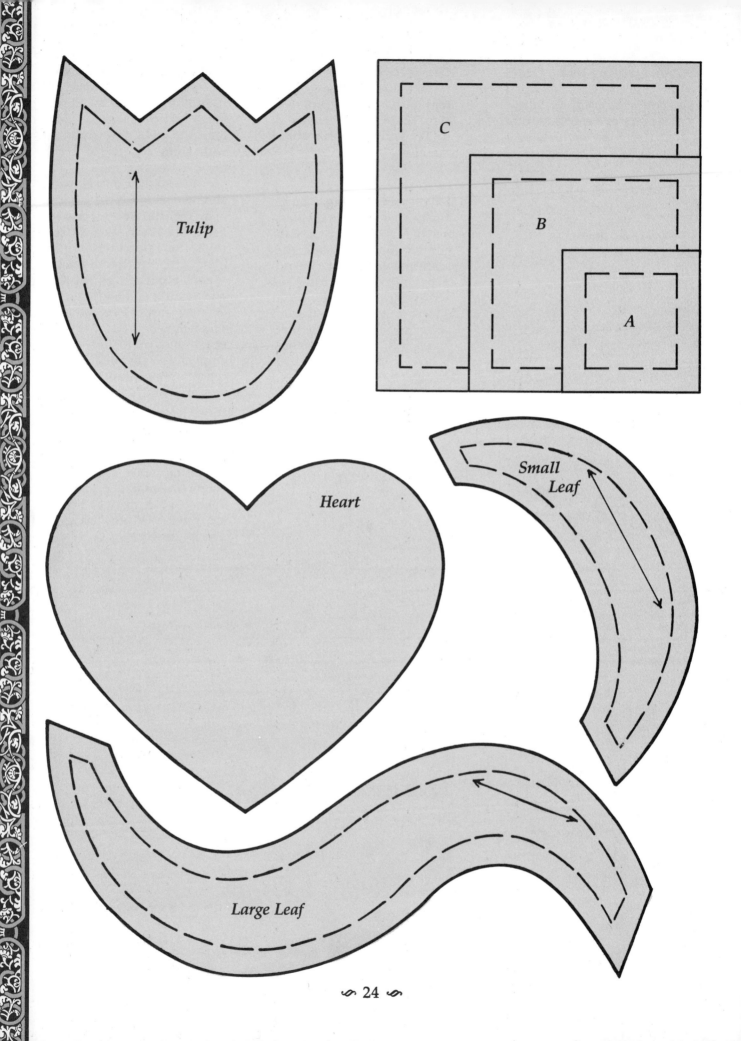

Tulip

C

B

A

Heart

Small Leaf

Large Leaf

GRANDMA'S LACE

"Inanimate objects do gather unto themselves something of the character of those who live among them, through association, and this alone makes heirlooms valuable. "

Lucy Larcom

A family treasure such as a lace tablecloth should be out for everyone to appreciate. Here we tell you how one such heirloom was made into a coverlet fit for a princess. Our lace piece measured 69" x 69" and had a delicate scalloped border. Below, we explain how we fashioned a light-weight quilt from blue satin, and sized it to let the lace border stand alone. However, the quilt is so simple, you can design it to fit your treasured heirloom any way you want. Or, if it's time to make an heirloom for the generations to come, find a new piece of lace that strikes your fancy. You could also show off your creativity by using lace squares instead of one whole piece. Just let your imagine do the work, and the result will be a charming way to display the best of your best for years to come.

1. **Measure lace.** Place lace piece on a flat surface. Measure length and width without the border and add $1/2$" to both measurements for seam allowance.

2. **Cut materials.** Cut 6 yards of blue satin into three 2-yard pieces. Then cut one of the 2-yard pieces in half lengthwise. Stitch one smaller piece to a 2-yard piece, matching right sides and selvage edges. Repeat. From these, cut two 67" x 67" pieces. Cut 6 yards of flannel into two 2-yard pieces. Then cut one of the 2-yard pieces in half lengthwise. Stitch one smaller piece to the 2-yard piece, matching right sides and selvage edges. Cut one 67" x 67" piece.

3. **Mark quilting lines.** Mark 45-degree diagonal lines $2^1/2$" apart over entire surface of one piece of satin. Repeat from opposite direction to make diamond pattern.

4. **Assemble quilt.** Baste flannel to wrong side of marked satin piece. With right sides of satin pieces together, stitch all edges, leaving a large opening. Trim flannel from seam allowances. Trim corners. Turn. Slipstitch opening closed.

5. **Quilt.** Quilt surface of satin quilt with matching thread.

6. **Complete the throw.** Sew matching ribbon to lace on inside edge of border using small running stitch. Center the lace over the unquilted piece. Slipstitch the quilt to the lace on all edges. Additional tacking to secure the lace may be desired.

PERFECT PEARLS

The hours I spent with thee, dear heart,
Are as a string of pearls to me....

Robert Cameron Rogers

QUILT:

Finished size: 68" x 86"

Fabrics needed:	Cut sizes:
Muslin: 12 yards	Twelve muslin hearts* Twelve $18^1/2$" x $18^1/2$" pieces Two 8" x $72^1/2$" border strips Two 8" x 68" border pieces Two $36^1/2$" x 88" backing strips 7 yards of 3"-wide bias for binding
Green print: $^1/2$ yard	Twelve of Template A*
Pink/white print: $^1/2$ yard	Twelve of Template B*
Floral print: $^1/2$ yard	Twelve of Template C*
Cream print: $^1/2$ yard	Twelve of Template D*
Pink print: $^1/2$ yard	Twelve of Template E*
Batting:	One 68" x 86" piece

Also needed:

$9^1/2$ yards of $^3/8$"-wide white lace
20 yards of Swiss embroidery with $1^1/2$"-wide pattern and entredeux edges
$11^1/2$ yards of $^5/8$"-wide eyelet beading
$11^1/2$ yards of $^3/8$"-wide pink satin ribbon
Embroidery floss: cream, pink, mauve, light green, dark green
Approximately 800 pearl beads

*See Step 1 of quilt before cutting.

PILLOW:

Finished size: $13^1/2$" x $13^1/2$" (without ruffle)

Fabrics needed:	Cut sizes:
Muslin: $2^1/2$ yards	One muslin heart* Two 14" x 14" pieces for top and back 3 yards of $4^1/2$"-wide bias for ruffle
Green print: scraps	One of Template A*
Pink/white print: scraps	One of Template B*
Floral print: scraps	One of Template C*
Cream print: scraps	One of Template D*
Pink print: scraps	One of Template E*
Batting: $^1/2$ yard	One 14" x 14" piece

Also needed:

$^7/8$ yard of $^3/8$"-wide white lace
3 yards of Swiss embroidery with $1^1/2$"-wide pattern and entredeux edges
$1^5/8$ yards of $^1/4$"-wide flat cream eyelet beading
3 yards of $^3/8$"-wide pink satin ribbon
Embroidery floss: cream, pink, mauve, light green, dark green
Approximately 70 pearl beads
16" pillow form

QUILT:

1. Prepare fabric. Make one Heart Pattern, adding $1/4"$ seam allowance. Cut twelve muslin hearts. Make templates from Heart Pattern. Trace templates onto each muslin heart for placement guide. Then, adding $1/4"$ seam allowances, use Templates A, B, C, D and E to cut fabric pieces.

2. Applique hearts. Pin green print A onto muslin heart, aligning outside edges. Match seam on pink/white B to print A; stitch through all layers. Open pink/white B (the outside edges of print pieces should align with edge of muslin heart.) Repeat to attach floral C, cream D and pink E. Repeat to make twelve hearts.

Cut twelve 27" pieces of $3/8"$-wide lace. Stitch one to outside edge of pieced heart with fullness toward center and with stitching line $1/4"$ from outside edge. Repeat for each heart.

Center and trace Heart Pattern without seam allowance in center of each muslin $18^{1}/2"$ x $18^{1}/2"$ piece. Applique hearts to muslin, placing gathered edge of lace outside heart.

3. Embroider hearts. Using two strands of floss, embroider seams as follows (Diagram 1):

A. Left diagonal seam: Blanket stitch ($1/2"$ apart) with dark green floss to make stems and cover seam; stitch lazy daisy stitch ($1/4"$ deep) with light green floss below each stem; stitch one French knot with cream floss above each stem; stitch five French knots with mauve floss surrounding each cream French knot.

B. Center vertical seam: Feather stitch ($1/2"$ apart) with light green floss over seam; stitch one French knot with mauve floss at end of each stem; stitch three lazy daisy stitches ($1/4"$ deep) with pink floss at top of each French knot.

C. Center diagonal seam: Blanket stitch ($1/2"$ apart) with dark green floss to make stems and cover seam; stitch three lazy daisy stitches ($1/4"$ deep) below and to each side of right angle in blanket stitch; stitch one

French knot with mauve floss at the top of each blanket stitch.

D. Right horizontal seam: Blanket stitch ($1/4"$ apart) with light green floss; lazy daisy stitch ($1/4"$ deep) with pink floss at right angle of every other blanket stitch; cross-stitch with cream floss over long stitch at right angle of remaining blanket stitches.

4. Assemble quilt. Stitch heart blocks together into four rows of three blocks. Stitch rows together.

5. Add border. Stitch 8" x $72^{1}/2"$ border strips to each side edge. Then stitch 8" x 68" border pieces to top and bottom edges.

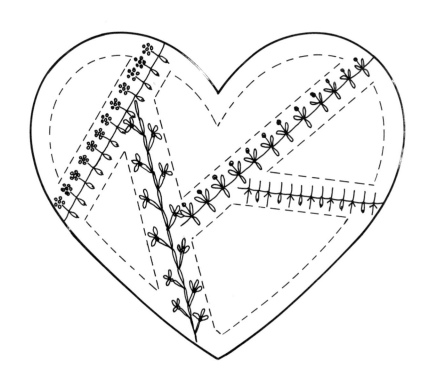

Diagram 1

6. **Attach trim**. Trim both entredeux edges from Swiss embroidery. Mark placement for Swiss embroidery trim 3" inside and parallel to each seam joining heart blocks (Diagram 2). Cut 58"-60" piece of trim and plan placement so mitered corners correspond as consistently as possible at each corner with the design in the trim. Slipstitch trim to quilt top. (In the model, six-strand pink embroidery floss was woven through the eyelet beading on both edges of the trim.)

Thread satin ribbon through eyelet beading. Stitch eyelet beading over horizontal seams. Then stitch eyelet beading over vertical seams, securing ribbon in eyelet beading and hiding raw ends.

7. **Mark quilting lines**. Mark 1"-wide grid of diamonds inside each Swiss embroidery trim. Mark Cable Pattern between all trim and eyelet beading. Repeat. Mark Border Pattern, adjusting if necessary, to make corners fit.

8. **Layer quilt**. Stitch two backing pieces together. Place the quilt backing wrong side up. Center batting and quilt top. Baste.

9. **Quilt**. Quilt around each heart with cream thread, stitching as close as possible to the appliqued edge and working through the lace. Also with the cream thread, quilt around edges of trim and eyelet beading. Quilt with pink thread inside and parallel to each seam on heart, not crossing any embroidery (Diagram 1). Also quilt all remaining marked lines with pink thread.

10. **Binding.** Bind all edges with muslin bias.

11. **Embellish quilt**. Stitch pearls to every intersection of diamond quilting lines on quilt top. Use a double strand of thread and work between the two layers of fabric. Secure all pearls with a stitch parallel to and on top of quilting lines.

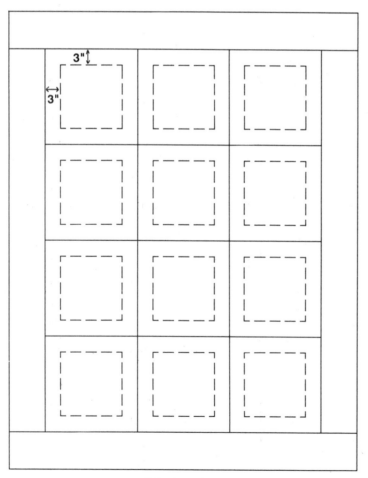

Diagram 2

PILLOW:

1. Prepare fabric. Complete Step 1 of quilt for one heart only.

2. Applique heart. Complete Step 2 of quilt.

3. Embroider heart. Complete Step 3 of quilt.

4. Mark quilting lines. Mark 1"-wide grid of diamonds on pillow top.

5. Add trim. Mark placement for eyelet beading about 1 ¼" from edges of fabric where grid lines intersect. Slipstitch edges of eyelet beading to muslin.

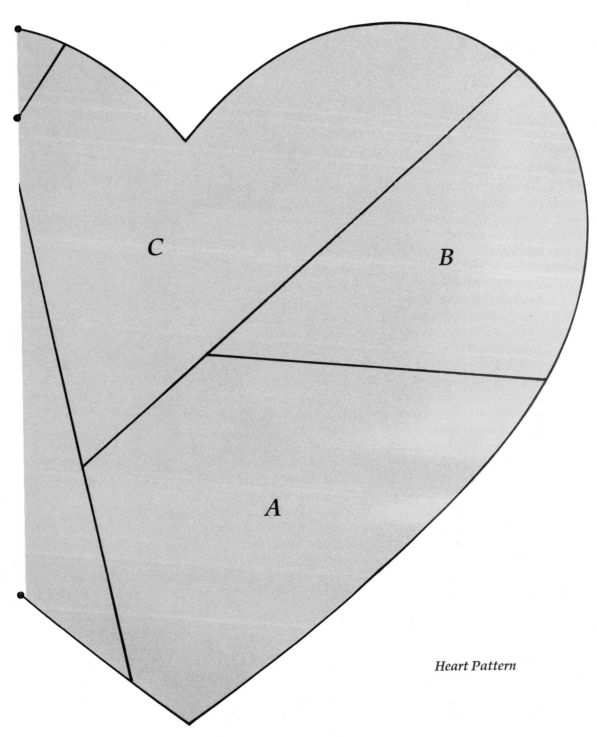

Heart Pattern

6. Layer pillow top. Place the pillow backing wrong side up. Center batting and pillow top. Baste.

7. Quilt. Complete Step 9 of quilt, except quilting around entredeux edges and eyelet beading. Instead, quilt with pink thread along inside edge of eyelet beading.

8. Embellish pillow. Complete Step 11 of quilt.

9. Complete pillow. Join ends of bias strip together. Fold in half to measure 2$\frac{1}{4}$" wide; press. Join ends of Swiss embroidery. Match raw edges of ruffle and Swiss embroidery. Stitch gathering threads through all layers parallel to and $\frac{1}{4}$" and $\frac{1}{2}$" from raw edges. Divide ruffle into fourths and mark. Place marks at each corner of pillow top. Gather ruffle to fit allowing extra fullness at corners. Stitch ruffle to edges of pillow top with fullness toward center.

Stitch pillow back to pillow top with right sides together leaving a large opening. Clip corners and turn. Insert pillow form. Slip-stitch opening closed.

10. Embellish pillow top. Complete Step 11 of quilt.

11. Add bows. Cut four 12" pieces of ribbon. Fold one piece into a bow. Tack to corner of eyelet beading. Attach three pearls close together in center of ribbon.

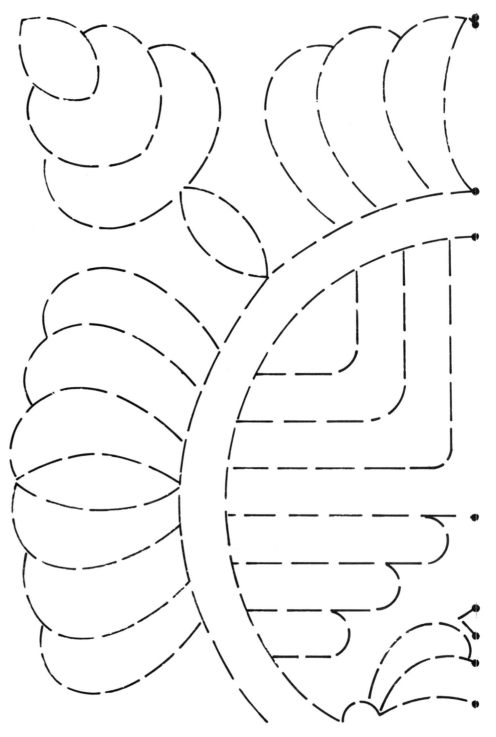

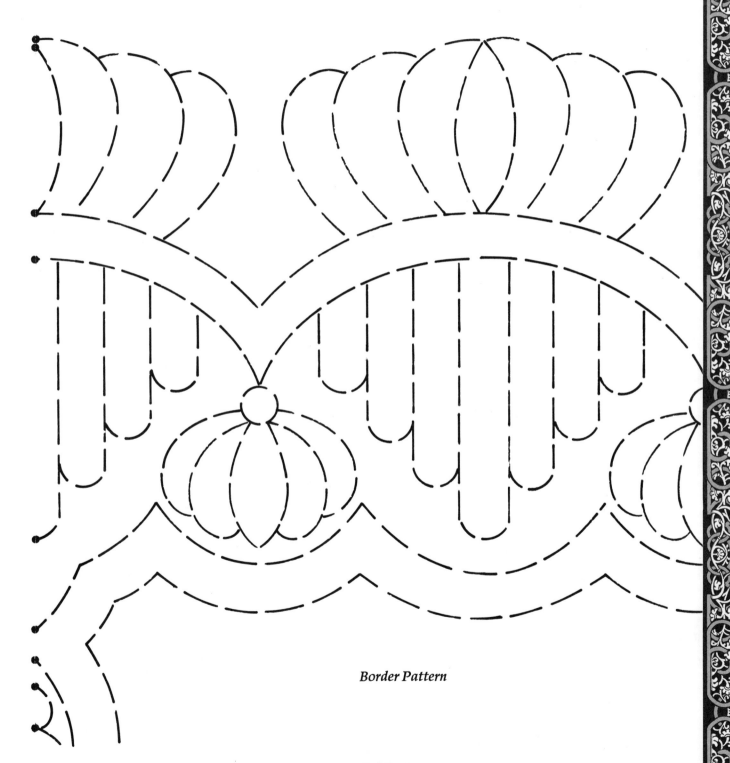

Border Pattern

Schematic

Cable Pattern

FANFARE

"How can a few notes of music, some paint on canvas, mere pieces of cloth sewn together, have this power to lift the human spirit? No one can explain this; it is the mystery of art."

Rose Wilder Lane

Finished size: 19^1/4" x 23"

Fabrics needed:	**Cut sizes:**
Cream taffeta with satin pattern: ^{5}/8 yard	One 17^1/2" x 22" background piece
Sage green moire taffeta: ^{5}/8 yard	One 3^1/2" x 13^1/2" piece One 5^1/2" x 13^1/2" piece 2^1/3 yards of 2^1/2"-wide bias strip for binding
Mauve linen: scraps	Two of Template A
Olive green linen: scraps	Two of Template B
Cream linen: ^{1}/4 yard	One 6^1/2" x 13^1/2" piece
Dark mauve moire taffeta: ^{1}/4 yard	One 16" x 7" piece
Muslin: ^{5}/8 yard	One 17^1/2" x 22" piece
Fleece: ^{5}/8 yard	One 17^1/2" x 22" piece

Also needed:

225 copper beads
21 ^{1}/4"-wide lavender buttons
Two ^{1}/2"-wide decorative buttons
Eleven ^{1}/2"-wide rectangular buttons
Olive thread for quilting
Thread to match fabrics

2^1/2 yards of ^{1}/2"-wide dark mauve picot satin ribbon
1 yard of ^{5}/8"-wide variegated mauve silk ribbon with gold edge
1^1/4 yards of ^{5}/8"-wide olive grosgrain ribbon with dot pattern

Note: Before marking any of these fabrics, test to be sure that the marks will come out. A hard lead pencil may be best.

1. **Applique panels to background.** Mark placement for four panels on cream background piece (Diagram 1). Cut two 13^1/$_2$" lengths of variegated ribbon. Pin gold edge of one length in vertical center of sage 3^1/$_2$" x 13^1/$_2$" piece. Pin plain edge of second length ^{1}/$_4$" from right edge of sage piece. Fold under seam allowances on all edges of sage piece and pin to cream background, securing ends of ribbon. Slipstitch sage piece to cream background, securing edge of second ribbon. Slipstitch remaining edges of ribbon to sage piece.

   For remaining three panels, fold under seam allowances on all edges and slipstitch to cream background (Diagram 1).

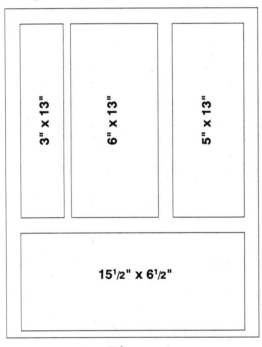

Diagram 1

2. **Applique fans and ribbons.** Fold under seam allowances on all mauve As and olive Bs and baste. Place the right angle of one olive B ^{1}/$_2$" from the left and bottom edges of the cream linen panel and applique. Place the second olive B ^{1}/$_2$" from the left and 7" from the bottom edge of the cream linen panel and applique. Applique mauve As over the green fans with straight edges ^{1}/$_4$" inside and parallel to olive fans.

   On dark mauve panel, mark horizontal placement for three ribbons 1^1/$_4$" apart with the first mark 1^1/$_2$" from the bottom edge. Mark vertical placement for seven ribbons a scant 2" apart. Cut three 16" lengths of dark mauve ribbon. Slipstitch to dark mauve panel where marked. Cut seven 6^1/$_2$" lengths of olive grosgrain ribbon. Slipstitch vertically over mauve ribbons where marked.

3. **Embellish panels.** Left sage panel: Mark placement for thirteen pairs of beads ^{1}/$_2$" apart at 1" intervals beginning ^{1}/$_2$" from top edge. Sew one bead on each mark.

   Center cream panel: Mark placement for beads on a ^{1}/$_2$" grid beginning ^{1}/$_4$" from both the left and bottom straight edges of mauve fan. Also mark placement for one bead ^{1}/$_2$" from point of scallop on olive fan. Sew one bead on each mark. Cut two 18" lengths of dark mauve ribbon. Fold into 3"-wide bows. Tack to lower left corner of each mauve fan. Sew one ^{1}/$_2$"-wide decorative button at center of each bow.

   Right sage panel: Mark placement for three columns of thirteen pairs of beads ^{1}/$_2$" from top edge. Sew one bead to each mark, omitting the center pair of beads on the center column. Mark placement for buttons, beginning the center column with one between the third and fourth pairs of beads, one in the center, and one between the ninth and tenth pairs of beads. Then mark button placement between columns of beads about 3^1/$_2$" apart beginning 1" from top edge. Sew one rectangular button to each mark.

   Dark mauve panel: Sew ^{1}/$_4$"-wide decorative buttons ^{1}/$_4$" above where ribbons intersect.

4. **Layer wallhanging.** Place the wallhanging backing wrong side up. Center the flannel and wallhanging top. Baste.

5. **Complete wallhanging.** Quilt with olive thread as close as possible to the mauve fans. Then echo quilt two rows ^{1}/$_4$" apart outside olive fans. Quilt as close as possible around each panel.

   Trim the backing and the fleece to match the wallhanging top. Bind the edges with the sage bias. Fold each corner toward the front of the wallhanging and secure with four beads placed ^{1}/$_4$" apart in a square pattern.

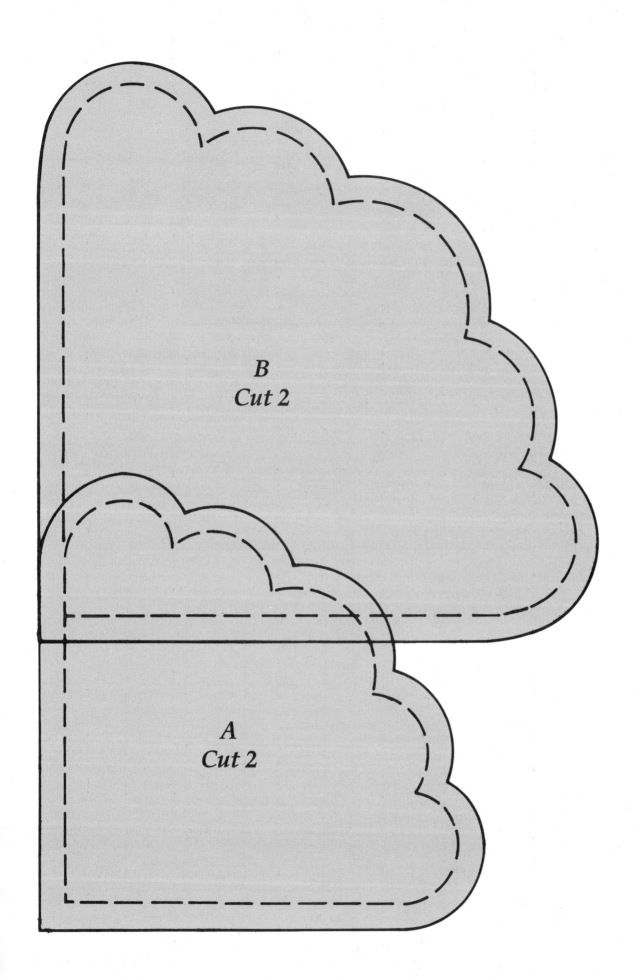

B
Cut 2

A
Cut 2

BUTTON SAMPLER

A thing of beauty is a joy forever:
Its loveliness increases; it will never
Pass into nothingness; but still will keep
A bower quiet for us, and a sleep
Full of dreams, and health, and quiet breathing.

John Keats

Fabrics needed:	Cut sizes:	Also needed:
Black satin: $1/4$ yard	One $6^1/2$" x $6^1/2$" piece Four of Template A	Sixteen assorted $1/2$"-wide black buttons with shanks
Black-on-black striped wool: $3/8$ yard	One 14" x 14" backing piece	2 yards of 1"-wide double-faced black satin ribbon
Black/white: scraps	Four of Template B	Dressmakers' chalk
Flannel: $3/8$ yard	One 10" x 10" piece	**Finished size:** 10" x 10"

1. **Mark quilting lines.** Mark horizontal and vertical centers of $6^1/2$"x$6^1/2$" black satin piece. Then mark parallel to and $1^1/4$" on both sides of center marks (Diagram 1).

2. **Construct sampler.** Layer the quilt backing wrong side up. Center flannel and sampler top. Fold backing to front, overlapping edges of black satin $1/4$". (Do not turn under raw edges.) Baste edges. Miter corners (Diagram 2). Slipstitch corner seams. Quilt on quilting lines with black thread. Quilt corners of binding; see Schematic.

3. **Add embellishments.** To add ribbon border, cut one 34" piece of ribbon. Place over edge of backing, beginning and ending on one corner, covering seam and overlapping onto black satin by $1/8$". Miter corners. Slipstitch edges and corner seams of ribbon.

To make yo-yos, sew running stitch $1/8$" from edge of black satin A. Gather tightly. Secure thread. Fold

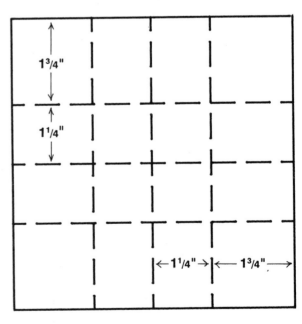

Diagram 1

 labels: $1^3/4$", $1^1/4$", $1^1/4$", $1^3/4$"

flat with gathering in center. Repeat with remaining black satin As and black/white Bs. Place center of one black/white yo-yo at outside corner of ribbon border. Tack. Center one black satin yo-yo over black/white yo-yo. Tack. Repeat at each corner.

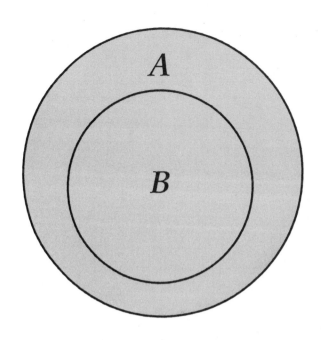

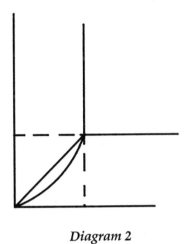

Diagram 2

Sew buttons onto black satin, centering the first four in center blocks. Sew remaining buttons $1^{1}/4$" from first four buttons.

To attach ribbon bow, tie 5"-wide bow in center of remaining ribbon. Place ends on back of sampler turning under raw edges. Slipstitch ribbon to back.

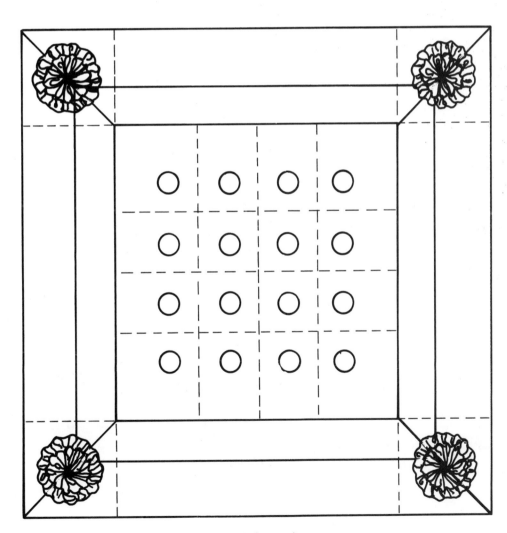

Schematic

Baby's Sleepytime Set

Baby's boat's a silver moon
Sailing in the sky
Sailing through a sea of sleep
While the stars go by

Sail, baby, sail
Far across the sea,
Only don't forget to sail
Back again to me

American Lullaby

BLANKET:

Finished size: 36" x 36"

One 36" x 36" piece of cream, medium-weight raw silk fabric
$1/4$ yard of cream cotton fabric
$4^1/2$ yards of 2"-wide cream satin blanket binding; matching thread
Floss: Nova rayon #166

PILLOW:

Finished size: 13" x 16"

One 26" x 18" piece of cream, medium-weight raw silk fabric
Floss: Nova rayon #166
$3/4$ yard of $3/8$"-wide cream trim
One 12" x 15" pillow

BLANKET:

1. Fold silk into fourths. Trace pattern, placing child's chin at center of fabric. Add $1/4$" seam allowance to patterns for moon and stars. Cut one moon and three stars from cotton fabric.

2. Applique moon and stars to silk.

3. Embroider edges of each appliqued piece in outline stitch. Embroider child in outline stitch. Embroider buttons with French knots. For child's face, separate one strand and outline stitch.

4. Stitch blanket binding to edges of silk, mitering the corners.

PILLOW:

1. Make template from Circle Pattern.

2. Fold silk to measure 13" x 18". Sew a French seam in one end and on the long edge. Turn. Fold 2" hem in open end. Slipstitch hem.

Diagram 1

3. Fold pillow case flat. Mark center of hemmed edge. Match center of circle to mark. Trace first circle 1/4" from hemmed edge. Overlap subsequent circles 1/4" and trace around entire edge, adjusting as needed to appear even at seam.

4. Feather stitch each circle, reversing direction from clockwise to counterclockwise with each (Diagram 1). Slipstitch to folded edge. Insert pillow.

Circle Pattern

APPLIQUED BOUQUET

"The flowers are nature's jewels, with whose wealth she decks her summer beauty."

George Croly

Finished size: 71¹/2" x 87¹/2"

Fabrics needed:

Cut sizes:

White: 10 yards

Twelve 16 ¹/2" x 16 ¹/2" pieces
Two 12" x 89" border strips
Two 12" x 74" border strips
Two 45" x 74" backing pieces
9 yards of 2"-wide bias for binding

Pink: ¹/2 yard   28 of Template A

Lavender: ¹/2 yard   28 of Template B

Yellow: ¹/4 yard   28 of Template B

Apricot: ¹/4 yard   28 of Template B

Blue: ¹/4 yard   28 of Template C

Green: ¹/4 yard   88 of Template D
                        140 of Template E

Lightweight batting: One 74" x 89" piece

Also needed:

White thread for construction and quilting
Embroidery floss for applique: pink, lavender, yellow, apricot,
    blue, green, black

1. **Embroider templates.**   Using one strand matching floss, stem stitch lines in all As, Bs and Cs. Using black thread, embroider French knots in centers of As and Bs.

2. **Applique blocks**. Trace Bouquet Pattern onto center of one 16¹/2" x 16¹/2" piece. (Connect pattern together by matching symbols). Baste leaves in place. Trim ¹/8" off exposed edges of leaf that tucks under pink center blossom in each block. Applique by working buttonhole stitch around edges. Baste flowers in place. Applique by working buttonhole stitch around edges. Applique cups at bottom of each flower. Outline stitch stems with green floss. Repeat to make twelve blocks.

3. Applique border. Mark center of each border strip. Position blossoms on one border strip, working with a pink and a lavender blossom on either side of the center mark and placing blossoms as desired (see photo). (The blue bud is always on the edge near the seam.) Position leaves. Mark stems. Applique all pieces. Outline stitch stems with green floss. Repeat to complete four border strips.

4. Assemble quilt. With the tops of all blocks facing the same direction, stitch four rows of three blocks together. Then stitch the four rows together; see Schematic.

5. Add border. Mark centers of each edge of quilt top. Also mark center of long inside edge of each border strip. Match center of long border strip to center of one side edge of quilt top. Stitch to within $1/4"$ of corner; backstitch. Repeat with remaining border strips. Miter the corners.

6. Mark quilting lines. Mark entire white background of quilt with diagonal lines 1" apart, making a diamond pattern.

7. Layer quilt. Place the quilt backing wrong side up. Center batting and quilt top. Baste.

8. Complete quilt. Quilt all marked lines with white thread. Also quilt outside each appliqued piece. Trim backing and batting to match the quilt top. Bind the edges with white bias.

Match with "X"s on page 59

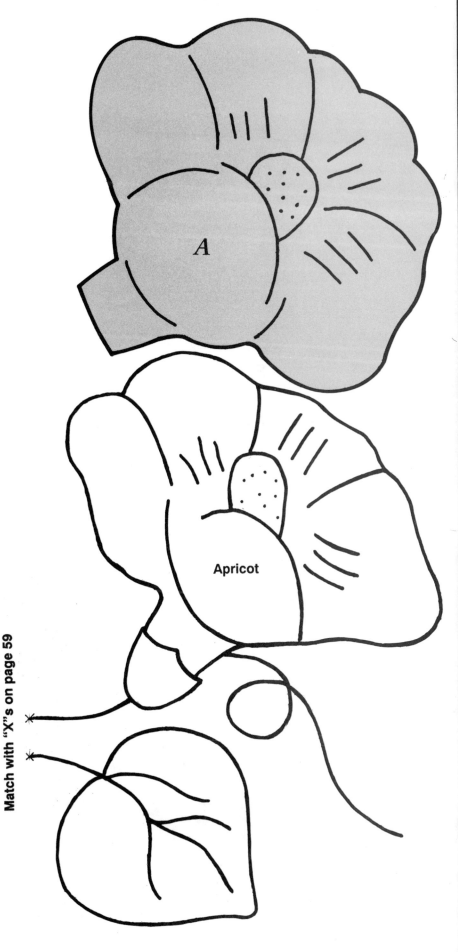

A

Apricot

Blue

B

Pink

Yellow

Bouquet Pattern

Lavender

C

D

E

Schematic

These projects are small enough that you may want to work them by hand. As a rule, all seam allowances are $^1/4$". However, if the blocks are so small that the $^1/4$" seam allowances touch on the back, they should be trimmed to $^1/8$" after each seam is sewn.

The porcelain jars (PC-3-00) are available from Anne Brinkley Design Co., 21 Ransom Road, Newton Centre, MA 02159.

The fabrics needed and cut sizes are listed individually. The finished size for all five designs is a $2^5/8$"-wide circle.

HEIRLOOM TREASURES

"And no matter how simple or traditional a pattern, the effect of a quilt is still absolutely original because no two people handle fabric and color the same way."

Beth Coutcheon

Satin Lid:

One 3"-wide round black porcelain jar
One 4" x 4" piece of unbleached muslin
Scraps of satin in seven different colors; matching thread
Assorted bugle and seed beads to match fabrics
Embroidery floss to match three fabrics
One $^1/2$"-wide brass button
Dressmakers' pen

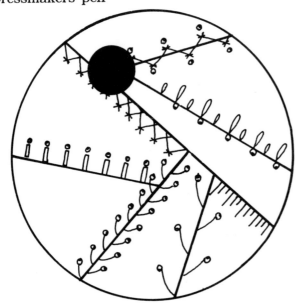

Satin Lid Pattern

1. Center and trace the acetate circle from jar onto the muslin. (It may be useful to trace the circle again after some or all of the fabric pieces are placed.) Make templates from Satin Lid Pattern. Place templates onto the fabrics and trace, adding a $^1/4$" seam allowance. Cut out.

2. Begin layering the fabrics by pinning one piece to the muslin. Layer the second and third pieces over the edges of the first at varying angles. Fold under $^1/8$" seam allowances on the edges which overlap the first piece. Slipstitch the folded edges with matching thread. Complete, using the four remaining fabrics; see pattern.

3. Embellish the seam lines with embroidery stitches; see Satin Lid Pattern. Add button and beads.

4. Cut on the pen line. Complete jar according to manufacturer's instructions.

Basket Block Lid:

One 3"-wide round black porcelain jar
Scraps of three print fabrics for basket
Scraps of purple fabric for background;
    matching thread
Three lavender seed beads
Dressmakers' chalk

1. Make templates from Basket Block Lid Pattern. Place the templates onto the fabrics and trace, adding a 1/4" seam allowance. Cut out.

2. Applique the handle to the background (Diagram 1). Stitch the pieces for the sides together (Diagram 2). Continue to piece the units (Diagram 3). Stitch the border strips to pieced block; see pattern. Sew three beads under handle; see pattern.

3. Center the acetate circle from jar over the design and trace onto the quilted piece. Cut on the pen line. Complete jar according to manufacturer's instructions.

Basket Block Lid Pattern

Diagram 1

Diagram 2

Diagram 3

Ribbon Lid:

One 3"-wide round black porcelain jar
One 4" x 4" piece of unbleached muslin
Four styles of ribbon in 2" to 3" lengths;
    matching threads
2" to 3" of 1³/4"-wide black velvet ribbon;
    matching thread
One ¹/2"-wide metal button
Three ³/16"-wide faceted metal beads
Dressmakers' pen

1. Center and trace the acetate circle from the jar over the muslin.

2. Arrange the ribbon in layers as desired (see Ribbon Lid Pattern) using the pen line as a guide. Tack the ribbon edges to the muslin. Add button and beads.

3. Cut on the pen line. Complete jar according to manufacturer's instructions.

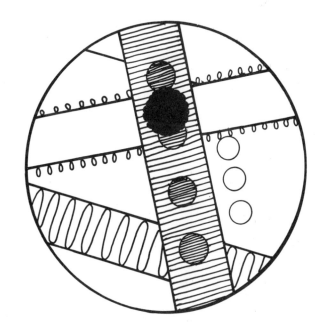

Ribbon Lid Pattern

Lace Lid Pattern

Lace Lid:

One 3"-wide round black porcelain jar
One 4" x 4" piece of unbleached muslin
Seven styles of white and cream lace in 2" to 3"
    lengths; matching thread
One decorative button
Three bugle beads to match button
Dressmakers' pen

1. Center and trace the acetate circle from jar over the muslin.

2. Arrange the lace in layers as desired (see Lace Lid Pattern) using the pen line as a guide. Tack the lace edges to the muslin. Add button and beads.

3. Cut on the pen line. Complete jar according to manufacturer's instructions.

House Block Lid:

One 3"-wide round black porcelain jar
Scraps of four print fabrics for house
Scraps of two solid-colored fabrics for chimneys,
    door and background
Thread to match background
White thread for quilting
One seed bead for doorknob
Dressmakers' chalk

1. Make templates from House Block Lid Pattern. Place the templates onto the fabrics and trace, adding a ¹/4" seam allowance. Cut out.

2. Stitch one chimney and one background piece together (Diagram 1). Repeat. Join the remaining background pieces to make a strip (Diagram 2). Complete the remaining strips (Diagrams 3 and 4).

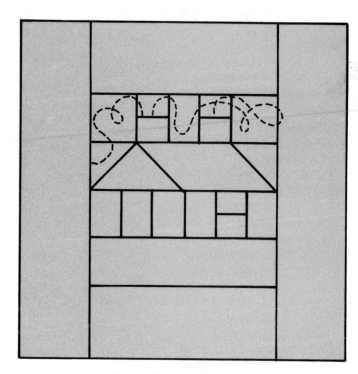

House Block Lid Pattern

3. Piece the strips together (Diagram 5) and add the border (Diagram 6). Press.

4. Quilt the smoke lines with white thread (see House Block Lid Pattern). Stitch the bead to the door.

5. Center the acetate circle from the jar over the design and trace onto the quilted piece. Cut on the pen line. Complete jar according to the manufacturer's instructions.

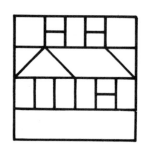

Diagram 5

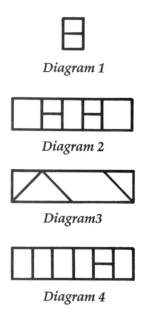

Diagram 1

Diagram 2

Diagram3

Diagram 4

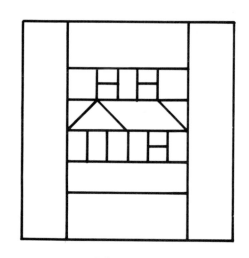

Diagram 6

CHRISTMAS GLOW

"Happy, happy Christmas, that can win us back to the delusions of our childish days, recall to the old man the pleasures of his youth, and transport the traveler back to his old fireside and quiet home!"

Charles Dickens

WALLHANGING:

Finished size: 20" x 20"

Fabrics needed:	Cut sizes:
Muslin: ¹/2 yard	One 18" x 18" piece
Red/green/metallic gold plaid: 1¹/4 yards	Five of Template A Three of Template B One 20" x 20" backing piece 2¹/2 yards of 1¹/2"-wide bias for binding
Green/gold/red print: ³/4 yard	Five of Template C Four 2¹/2" x 20¹/2" border strips One 18" x 18" piece Four 2¹/2" x 20¹/2" border strips
Green: ¹/8 yard	Sixteen of Template B
Red: ¹/8 yard	Four 1" x 20¹/2" binding strips
Polyester fleece	One 20" x 20" piece

Also needed:

Dark green thread Gold metallic thread Two-ply gold metallic thread	75 3-mm gold beads Seven 5-mm gold beads Five ¹/4" gold oval beads Dressmakers' chalk

PILLOW:

Finished size: 14" x 14" without ruffle

Fabrics needed:	Cut sizes:
Muslin: 1¹/2 yards	Two 14¹/2" x 14¹/2" pieces Three yards of 5"-wide bias for ruffle
Red/green/metallic gold plaid: ³/4 yard	Four of Template B One 14¹/2" x 14¹/2" piece for pillow back 60" of 1"-wide bias for corded piping
Green: scraps	Eight of Template B
Polyester fleece:	One 14¹/2" x 14¹/2" piece

Also needed:

Dark green thread
Gold metallic thread
Cream thread for construction
2 yards of small cording
24 3-mm gold beads
One 5-mm gold bead
One 16" x 16" pillow form
Dressmakers' chalk

MUSLIN ORNAMENT:

Finished size: 6" long

Fabrics needed:	Cut sizes:
Muslin: 8" x 8" piece	Two of Template A
Green: scraps	Two of Template B

Also needed:

Gold metallic thread	Six 3-mm gold beads
Cream thread for construction	Three 5-mm gold beads
Dark green thread	Two 1/4" gold oval beads
Nylon thread	Stuffing
3/4 yard of gold cord	

PLAID ORNAMENT:

Finished size: 7" long

Fabrics needed:	Cut sizes:
Muslin: 8" x 8" piece	Two of Template A (do not cut out center)
Red/green/metallic gold plaid: 8" x 8" piece	Two of Template A Two of Template B
Green/gold/red print: scraps	Two of Template C

Also needed:

Gold metallic thread	Two 5-mm gold beads
Dark green thread	Two 1/4" gold oval beads
3/4 yard of gold cord	Stuffing
Nylon thread	
25 3-mm gold beads	

STOCKING:

Finished size: 12" long

Fabrics needed:	Cut sizes:
Muslin: scraps	One of Template G Two stocking pieces
Red/green/metallic gold plaid: 1/2 yard	1 1/2 yards of 1"-wide bias for corded piping 1 1/4 yards of 1 3/4"-wide bias for loop and bow One of Template D
Green/gold/red print: 3/8 yard	Two stocking pieces One of Template F
Green: scraps	Four of Template E
Red: 3/8 yard	Two stocking pieces for lining
Polyester fleece:	Two stocking pieces

Also needed:

Gold metallic thread
Dark green thread
Two-ply gold metallic thread
1 yard of small cording
3/8 yard of gold cord
Twenty 3-mm gold beads
Two 5-mm gold beads
One 1/4" gold oval bead
Dressmakers' chalk

WALLHANGING:

1. Prepare muslin. Mark 1" inside all four edges of muslin piece. Then mark 2" grid inside the lines (Diagram 1). Trim $1/4$" from outside edges of Templates A, B and C. Beginning in upper left corner, trace four rows of four Template As onto muslin for placement guide (Diagram 2). Trace Templates B and C; see Wallhanging Schematic for placement.

2. Applique wallhanging top. Applique outside and inside edges of five red plaid As. Applique green print Cs to center of each red plaid A. Applique three red plaid Bs; see photo. Applique sixteen green Bs; see photo.

3. Add border. Repeat marking procedure for grid (see Step 1) on 18" x 18" green print using chalk. Then, using Template A as a pattern, mark the scalloped border line using grid for placement.

Place green print piece right side up over right side of muslin/ applique piece, matching outsides and intersections of grid lines. (Stick pin straight through both layers and raise top layer to check work.) Baste outside edges only.

Carefully cutting through green print layer only, cut $1/4$" inside scalloped border line. Cut 2" to 3" at a time. Applique edge. Repeat process until border is complete.

Trim both layers $1/4$" outside grid to make $16^1/2$" x $16^1/2$" appliqued wallhanging top. Stitch border strips to wallhanging top, mitering the corners.

4. Embroider wallhanging top. Using one strand of gold metallic thread, complete these steps:

a. Make eight straight stitches into center of each green print C (Diagram 3).

b. Attach 3-mm beads in center and at outside ends of each straight stitch (Diagram 3).

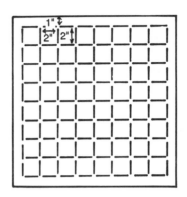

Diagram 1

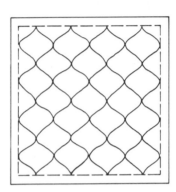

Diagram 2

Wallhanging Schematic

Diagram 3

c. Blanket stitch around each green B (Diagram 4).

d. Work lazy daisy and straight stitches in centers of each green B (Diagram 4).

e. Attach 3-mm beads in center (Diagram 4).

Diagram 4

f. Trace three-loop pattern above each red plaid A (Diagram 5).

g. Couch two-ply gold thread over three-loop pattern.

h. Attach one 5-mm bead, one oval bead and two 3-mm beads at top point of each red plaid A (Diagram 5).

i. Where red plaid As and Bs intersect, attach one 3-mm bead.

j. On two bottom plaid As, attach one 5-mm bead, then attach one 3-mm bead below it.

Diagram 5

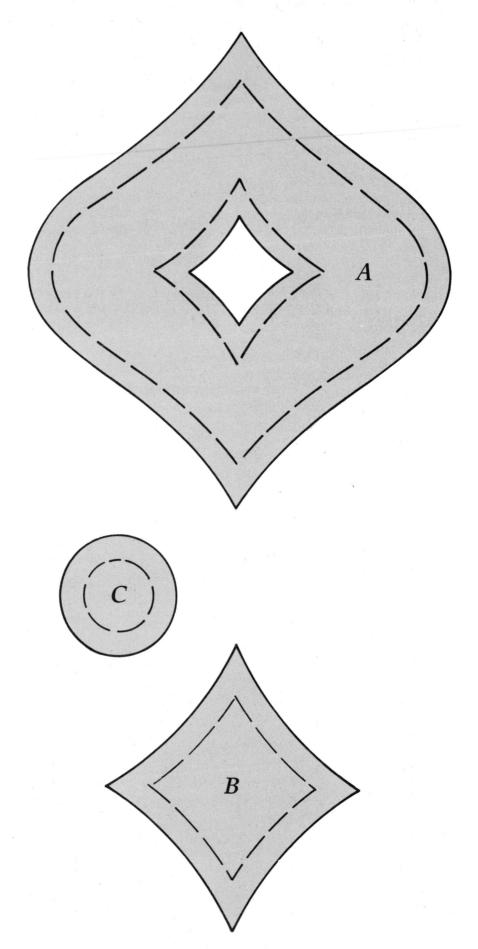

5. Mark quilting lines. Trace Template A onto border (see Wallhanging Schematic). Trace Template B in center of each A.

6. Layer wallhanging. Place the wallhanging backing wrong side up. Center the fleece and wallhanging top. Baste.

7. Complete wallhanging. Quilt with dark green thread on all marked lines of Template As and Bs and around edges of applique pieces.

8. Bind wallhanging. Fold red fabric in half to measure $3/8$"-wide. Press. Baste to edge of wallhanging, folding corners to miter. Bind wallhanging with plaid bias strip.

PILLOW:

1. Applique pillow top. Fold one $14^1/2$" x $14^1/2$" muslin piece into quarters. Mark folds. Then mark diagonal lines from corner to corner. Trace pillow pattern onto pillow top, including quilting lines, using quarter marks as guides. Applique dark green Bs to pillow top; see photo. Applique plaid Bs; see photo.

2. Embroider pillow top. Using one strand of metallic gold thread, complete Steps 4c and 4d of wallhanging instructions.

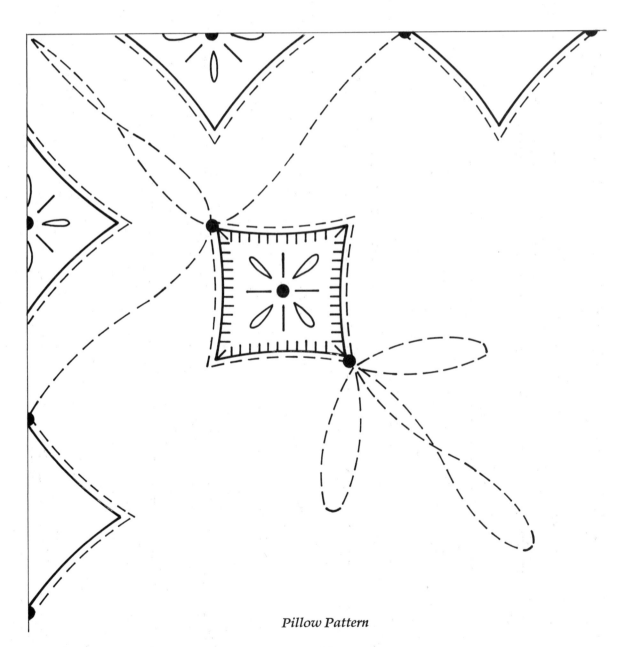

Pillow Pattern

3. Quilt pillow top. Layer second $14^{1}/_{2}$" x $14^{1}/_{2}$" muslin piece, fleece and pillow top. Baste. Quilt all lines with dark green thread; see pattern.

4. Add beads. Attach eight 3-mm beads to center of each green B, and to top and bottom points of outside row of eight Bs; see pattern. Attach 5-mm bead to center of pillow.

5. Complete pillow. Make 60" of corded piping from red plaid bias. Stitch to right side of pillow top, rounding corners. Stitch 5" ends of ruffle piece together. Fold ruffle to measure $2^{1}/_{2}$" wide.

Pin box pleats in ruffle (Diagram 6), adding extra fullness in corners. Place right side of ruffle over pillow top, aligning raw edges with corded piping and top. Stitch ruffle to pillow top, sewing on stitching line of corded piping. Stitch pillow front and back together, leaving large opening in one edge. Insert pillow form. Slipstitch opening closed.

$1^{3}/_{4}$"

$^{1}/_{2}$" $^{1}/_{2}$"

Diagram 6

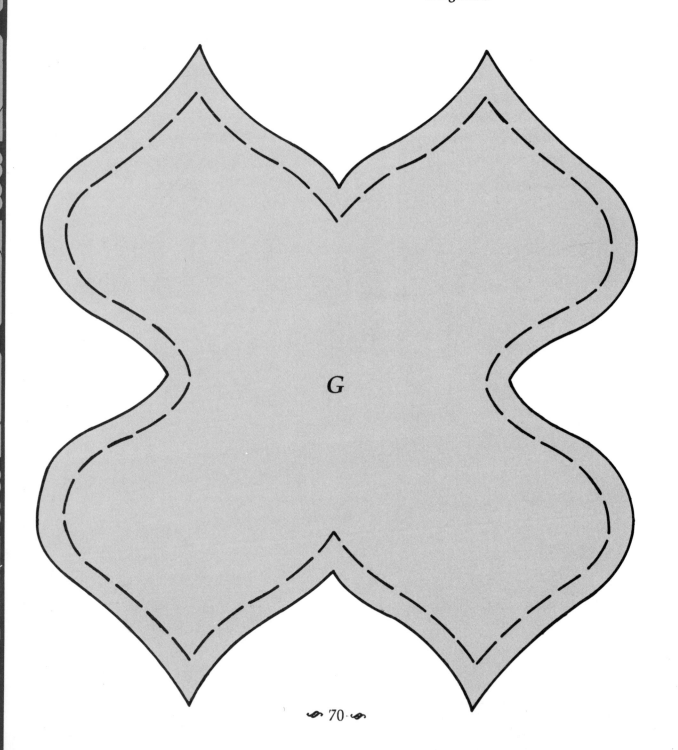

G

STOCKING:

1. **Applique stocking.** Applique muslin G 2" from top edge of one green print stocking. Then applique inside and outside edges of plaid D to center of muslin G. Applique print F to center of muslin G. Applique four green Es; see photo.

2. **Embroider stocking.** Using one strand of metallic gold thread, complete Step 4a of wallhanging in green print F; Step 4b; Step 4c around each green E; Step 4d in each green E; Steps 4f and 4g above plaid D. Then trace the twisted loop pattern (Diagram 7) above the two points of the muslin G. Chain stitch twisted loop pattern. Attach one 3-mm bead to top and bottom of each muslin design. Attach one 5-mm bead to top and bottom of red plaid D. Vertically attach oval bead above top 5-mm bead.

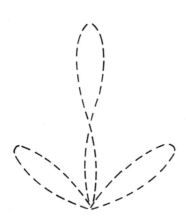

Diagram 7

3. **Mark quilting lines.** Trim $1/4$" from outside edge of Template D. Trace outside edge of Template D onto stocking front, beginning by fitting it around the appliqued G. Repeat to fill stocking front. Also mark repeats of Template D to fill stocking back.

4. **Layer stocking pieces.** Center one muslin piece, one fleece piece and stocking front. Baste. Repeat for back. Quilt stocking front by hand with dark green thread. Also quilt around all edges of plaid D and each green E. Quilt stocking back either by hand or machine.

5. **Complete stocking.** Make one yard of corded piping from 1"-wide plaid bias strip. Set aside remaining bias. Stitch corded piping to stocking

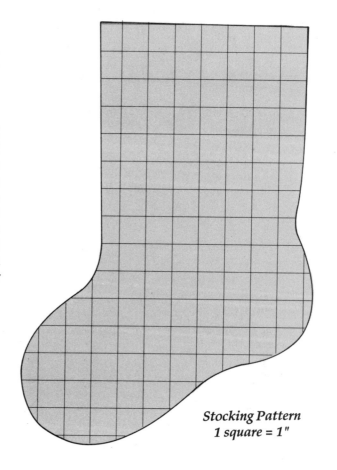

Stocking Pattern
1 square = 1"

D

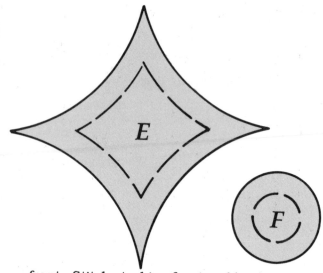

front. Stitch stocking front and back together on stitching line of corded piping. Turn. Stitch red lining pieces together. Place lining inside stocking, aligning top edges and side seams. Stitch remaining 1"-wide bias to top of stocking, securing lining in seam. Fold bias double to inside and slipstitch.

Fold 1³/4"-wide bias to measure ⁷/8" wide. Stitch long edge. Turn. Cut one 4" piece. Fold to make 2" loop. Slipstitch to inside of stocking on back seam, tucking ends under. Cut one 2" piece. Fold remaining bias into 4"-wide loops and place 2" piece around center. Slipstitch piece to bow, then bow to stocking. Fold gold cord into 4"-wide bow and slide under 2" piece.

Couch two-play gold metallic thread with gold thread to front of stocking, stitching in-the-ditch between the corded piping and stocking front.

MUSLIN ORNAMENT:

1. **Applique ornament.** Applique one green B to center of muslin A. Repeat for back.

2. **Embroider ornament.** Using one strand of metallic gold thread, complete Steps 4c, 4d, and 4e of wallhanging instructions. Quilt by hand with dark green thread on muslin. Repeat for back.

3. **Construct ornament.** Stitch front and back muslin As together leaving an opening. Turn. Stuff moderately. Slipstitch opening closed.

Couch gold cord with gold thread to seam line of muslin A, beginning at the top, working down one side, making a 1" loop at bottom and then working up second side; do not cut cord. Fold cord into three loops similar to Diagram 5. Secure end of cord.

Sew two 3-mm beads, one 5-mm bead and one oval bead to both front and back of ornament at top. Sew one 5-mm bead to bottom of muslin A.

Make loop for hanging with nylon thread. Attach to top.

PLAID ORNAMENT:

1. **Applique ornament.** Applique inside edge of red plaid A over muslin A, making opening to expose muslin in center. Applique green print C to center. Repeat for ornament back.

2. **Embroider ornament.** Using one strand of gold metallic thread, complete Steps 4a and 4b of wallhanging instruction. Trim ¹/4" from Template B. Center Template B over muslin and trace. Repeat for back. Quilt by hand with dark green thread on muslin. Repeat for back.

3. **Construct ornament.** Stitch front and back red plaid As with right sides together leaving an opening. Turn. Stuff moderately. Slipstitch opening closed. Stitch together two red plaid Bs leaving a small opening. Turn. Stuff moderately. Slipstitch opening closed. Tack B to bottom of A.

Couch gold cord with gold metallic thread to seam line of red plaid A and B, beginning at the top, working down one side of A then one side of B and back up B, then A; do not cut cord. Fold cord into three loops similar to Diagram 5. Secure end of cord.

Sew two 3-mm beads, one 5-mm bead and one oval bead to both front and back of ornament at top. Sew one 3-mm bead to both front and back where red plaid A and B are tacked together. Sew one bead to bottom of red plaid B.

Make loop for hanging with nylon thread. Attach to top.

Finished size: 15" x 25¹/₂"

Fabrics needed: Cut sizes:

Five assorted prints: (see individual steps)
  scraps

Dusty blue: scraps   (see individual steps)

Sage green: scraps   (see individual steps)

Gray print: 1 yard   One 17" x 27" backing
                              piece

                            Two 14¹/₂" x 4¹/₂"
                              pieces for casing
                            (see individual steps for
                              additional pieces)

Metallic gold fabric: (see individual steps)
  ¹/₈ yard

Tan/black print: Two yards of 2¹/₄"-wide
  1 yard   bias for binding
                            (see individual steps for
                              additional pieces)

Polyester fleece: One 17" x 27" piece
  ³/₄ yard

Also needed:

Gold thread for quilting
Gray thread for construction
Assorted beads
Two bird beads
One 15"-long brass curtain rod with finial
One 22" length of gold cord

Victorian Organizer

"If you want a golden rule that will fit everybody, this is it: Have nothing in your houses that you do not know to be useful, or believe to be beautiful."

William Morris

---

1. Construct top section. Cut the following pieces:

Four 1" x 7¹/₂" gold pieces
Two 1" x 7¹/₂" red print pieces
Two 1" x 7¹/₂" melon print pieces
One 2¹/₂" x 4" gray print piece
Two 1¹/₂" x 4" tan/black print pieces
Two 2³/₄" x 4" sage pieces

Join the 7¹/₂" pieces in this order: gold, red print, gold, melon print, gold, red print, gold, melon print. Cut into two 3³/₄" pieces of horizontally pieced strips.

Stitch together pieces of top section in this order: sage, pieced strips, tan/black print, gray print, tan/black print, pieced strips, sage (Diagram 1).

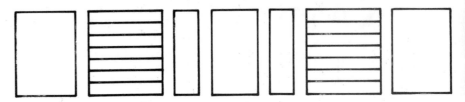

Diagram 1

2. Construct upper pocket section. Cut the following pieces:

One 1½" x 8" dusty blue piece
Two ¾" x 8" melon print pieces
Two 2¼" x 8" light blue print pieces
One 1½" x 8" gold piece
Two 1¾" x 8" navy print pieces
Two 1" x 8" melon/white stripe pieces
Four 7½" x 7½" gray print pieces

Join the 8" pieces in this order: light blue print, melon print, dusty blue, melon print and light blue print. Cut into two 4" pieces of horizontally pieced strips.

Join the remaining 8" pieces in this order: melon/white stripe, navy print, gold, navy print, melon/white stripe. Cut into two 4" pieces of horizontally pieced strips.

Place Template A on one pieced stripe piece, aligning arrow with center of middle piece of fabric. Cut four pieces like Template A. Stitch sides of two matching pieces together for top of pocket front (Diagram 2). Repeat for bottom of pocket front (Diagram 3). Join the top and bottom halves.

Place one 7½"x7½" gray print piece and pocket front with right sides together. Stitch edges of diamond opening between seams, backstitching at each seam and not sewing into seam

allowance (Diagram 4). Cut diamond opening in gray print fabric to match edges of opening. Clip gray print in seam allowance at each corner of opening. Turn gray print through diamond opening. Baste gray print to pocket front.

Sandwich pocket front piece with diamond opening between the right sides of two gray print pieces. Stitch top 7½" edges together. Turn so gray print piece shows through diamond opening (Diagram 5). Pin pocket front over right side of remaining gray print piece. Stitch one charcoal piece to each 6½" side of pocket, securing all layers in seams (Diagram 6).

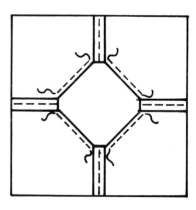

Diagram 4

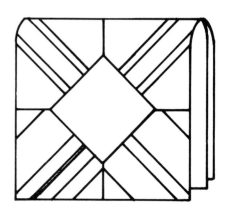

Diagram 5

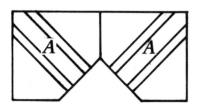

Diagram 2

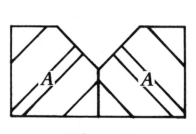

Diagram 3

Diagram 6

3. Construct middle pocket section. Cut the following pieces:

One 1¹/2" x 4" tan/black print piece
One 1¹/2" x 4" sage piece
One 1" x 4" melon/white stripe piece
One 1" x 6" gold piece
One 1" x 6" navy print piece
One 2¹/2" x 3" melon print piece
One 3" x 7¹/2" gray print piece

Join the 4" pieces in this order: tan/black print, sage, melon/white stripe. Cut into two 2" lengths. Join the 6" pieces of gold and navy print. Cut into two 3" lengths. Join the pieces of pocket front in this order: 2" pieced strips, 3" pieced strips, melon print piece, 3" pieced strips, 2" pieced strips (Diagram 7). Stitch gray print piece to pocket front with right sides together. Set small pocket aside.

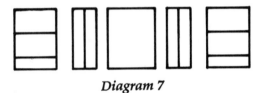

Diagram 7

4. Construct lower pocket section. Cut the following pieces:

One 1¹/4" x 8" melon print piece
One 1³/8" x 8" tan/black print piece
One red print of Template B
One 1" x 10" tan/black print piece
Two 1" x 10" gold pieces
One 1" x 10" red print piece
One 1" x 10" melon print piece
One 1¹/2" x 10" sage piece
One 1¹/2" x 7¹/2" navy print piece
One 1¹/4" x 7¹/2" melon/white stripe piece
Two ⁷/8" x 7¹/2" gold pieces
One 2³/8" x 7¹/2" light blue print piece
One 1¹/2" x 7¹/2" sage piece
One 7¹/2" x 7¹/2" gray print piece

Join the 8" pieces of melon and tan/black prints. Cut one piece like Template C with the melon on top; reverse template and cut second piece. Stitch one pieced C to each diagonal edge of red print B (Diagram 8).

Diagram 8

Join the 10" pieces in this order: tan/black print, gold, red print, gold, melon print, sage. Cut one piece like Template E with the tan/black on the left; reverse template and cut second piece.

Join the 7¹/2" pieces in this order: melon/white stripe, gold, light blue print, gold, sage. Cut one like Template D with the sage on top. Stitch the 7¹/2" piece of navy print to the bottom of pieced D.

Join pieced E/D/E (Diagram 9). Then stitch C/B/C to E/D/E to complete pocket front. Stitch gray print piece to top edge of pocket front with right sides together. Turn.

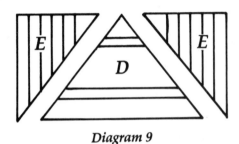

Diagram 9

5. Complete lower section. Cut the following pieces:

One 1¹/2" x 9" gold piece
One 3" x 7¹/2" gray print piece
One 7¹/2" x 7¹/2" gray print piece
One 1¹/2" x 7¹/2" navy print piece
One 9" x 6⁵/8" gray print piece
One 9" x 2¹/8" gray print piece
One 9" x 1¹/2" gray print piece
Two 9" x ⁷/8" gold pieces
One 8¹/2" x 5" charcoal print piece

Stitch 1¹/2" x 9" gold piece to bottom edge of upper pocket section, with right sides together, matching centers and securing all layers in seam.

Stitch 3" x 7¹/2" gray print piece to gold piece at bottom of upper pocket section. Pin middle pocket to right side of 3" x 7¹/2" gray print piece, aligning bottom edges. Stitch 7¹/2" x 7¹/2" gray print piece to bottom edge of middle section, with right sides together, matching centers and securing all layers in seam.

Pin lower pocket to right side of 7¹/2" x 7¹/2" gray print piece, aligning bottom edges. Stitch 1¹/2" x 7¹/2" navy print piece to bottom edge of lower pocket, with right sides together, matching centers and securing all layers in seam. Set aside middle/lower pocket section.

Join the three remaining gray print pieces with gold strips between (Diagram 10). Cut 9" edge to make two pieces 4$\frac{1}{2}$" wide. Stitch one to each side of middle/lower pocket section, securing all layers in seam.

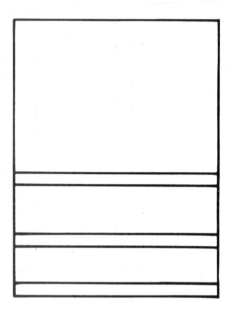

Diagram 10

Stitch 8$\frac{1}{2}$" x 5" charcoal print piece to bottom edge of wallhanging with right sides together and matching centers.

6. Attach casing. Cut one 28" x 4$\frac{1}{2}$" strip. Stitch short ends of casing pieces with right sides together. Turn. Fold to measure 14" x 4$\frac{1}{4}$". Center on top edge of wallhanging with right sides together and all raw edges matching. Stitch.

7. Layer wallhanging. Cut one 17" x 27" piece of gray print for wallhanging backing. Place the backing wrong side up. Center the fleece and wallhanging top. Baste. Center Wallhanging Pattern over wallhanging. Cut out through all layers.

8. Complete wallhanging. Bind side and bottom edges with tan/black print bias, mitering corners carefully. Turn under $\frac{1}{4}$" of backing on top edge and slipstitch. Quilt with gold thread in the larger pieces, following seams or pattern of print, and as desired for decoration.

9. Embellish wallhanging. String beads in a random pattern to make two 1" lengths with bird beads on ends. Attach to upper left and right corner blocks. String two 9" lengths, two 7$\frac{1}{2}$" lengths and two 6$\frac{3}{4}$" lengths. Attach to sides, secure to binding (see photo). String one 5$\frac{1}{2}$" and one 3" length. Attach to center of lower pocket. String six 3" lengths. Attach three to each lower corner.

Insert rod and hang with gold cord.

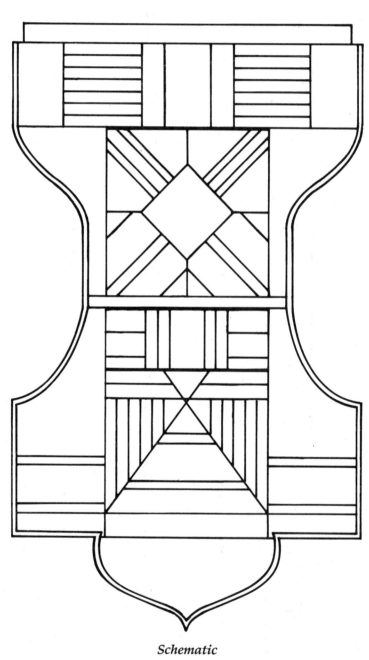

Schematic

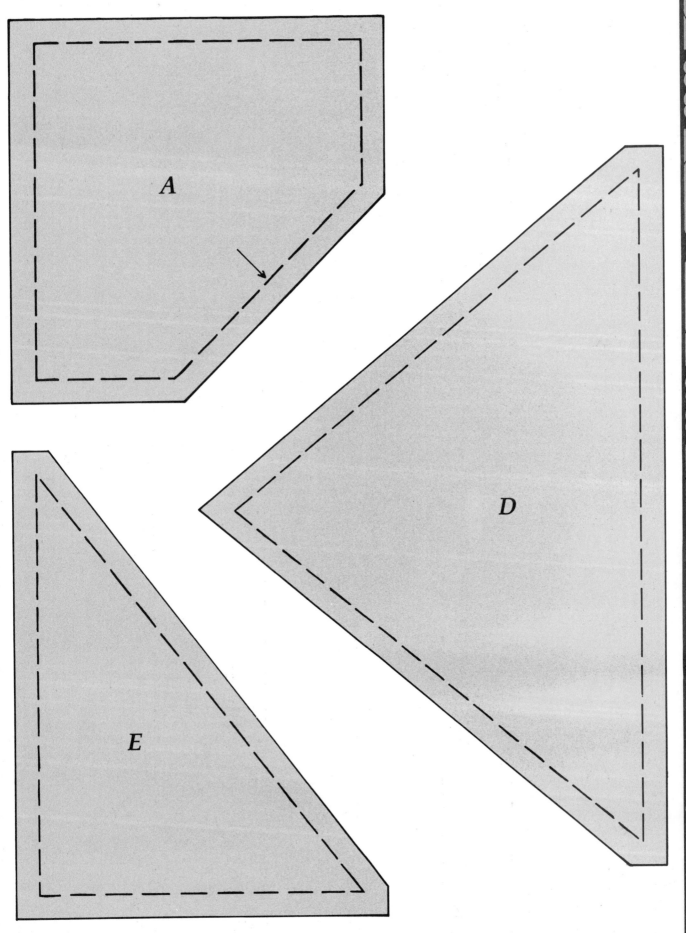

A

D

E

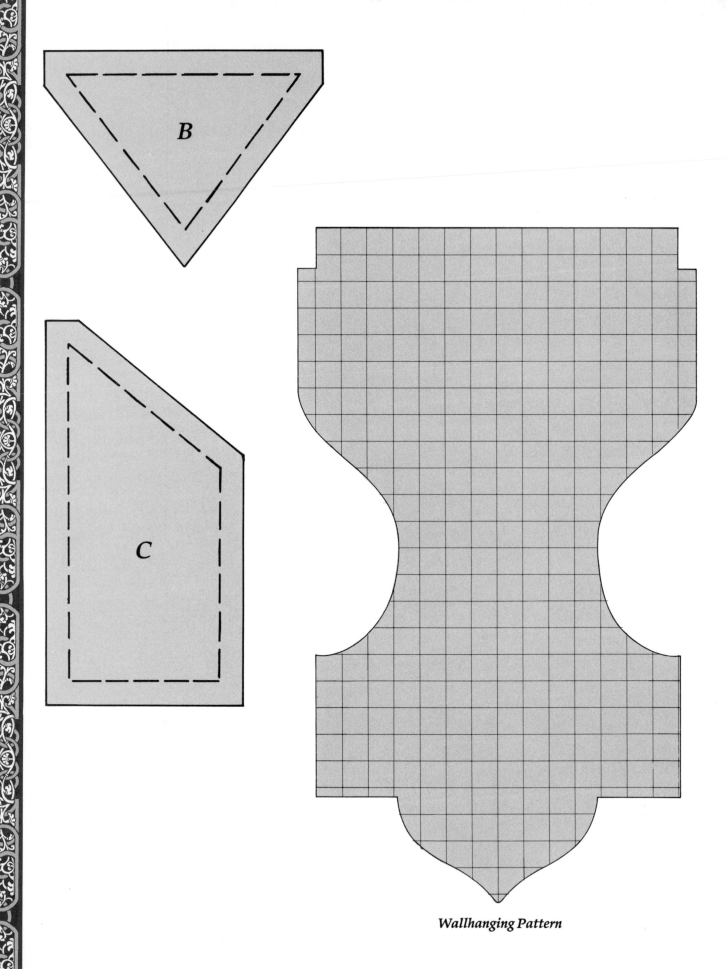

Wallhanging Pattern

BRIER ROSE

"One comes back to these old-fashioned roses as one does to music and old poetry. A garden needs old associations, old fragrances, as a home needs things that have been lived with."

Marion Page

QUILT:

Finished size: 26" x 33"

Fabrics needed: **Cut sizes:**

Rose: 1 yard
- 22 of Template B
- 22 of Template C
- $3^1/2$ yards of 2"-wide bias for binding

Green print: 1/4 yard
- 132 of Template D

Muslin: $2^1/4$ yards
- 22 of Template A
- 66 of Template B
- 132 of Template D
- Twenty of Template E
- Three of Template F
- Two $2^1/2$" x $16^1/2$" pieces
- Two $3^1/2$" x $16^1/2$" pieces
- Two $1^1/2$" x $33^1/2$" border strips
- Two $1^1/2$" x $26^1/2$" border strips
- One 30" x 36" backing piece

Polyester fleece: 1 yard
- One 30" x 36" piece

Also needed:

Rose thread for quilting
Cream thread for construction

BASKET LID:

Finished size: $5^1/2$" x $5^1/2$"

Fabrics needed: **Cut sizes:**

Rose: scraps
- Four of Template C
- 27" of $1^1/4$"-wide bias strips for corded piping

Green print: scraps
- Eight of Template D

Muslin: scraps
- One of Template F
- Eight of Template D

Fleece: scraps
- One 6" x 6" piece

Also needed:

One $5^1/2$" square reed basket with lid
Rose thread for quilting
$3/4$ yard of small cording
$3/4$ yard of ecru lace trim
Small amount of polyester stuffing

PIN CUSHION:

Finished size: $3^1/2$" x $3^1/2$"

See the individual project for materials needed.

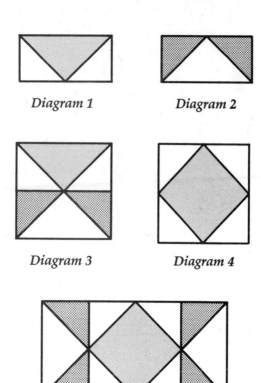

Diagram 1   *Diagram 2*

Diagram 3   *Diagram 4*

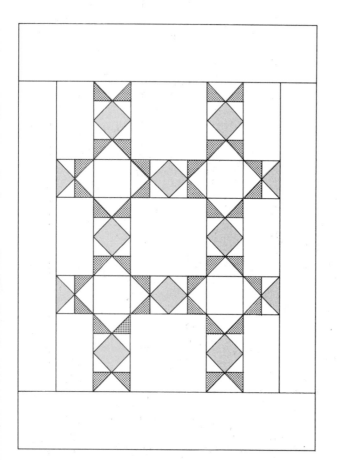

Diagram 5

Diagram 7

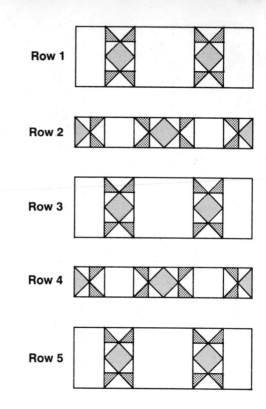

Row 1

Row 2

Row 3

Row 4

Row 5

Diagram 6

1. Construct 22 rosebud blocks. Stitch two muslin Ds to each diagonal edge of rose B (Diagram 1). Repeat to make 22 sets. To make leaves, stitch two green print Ds to each diagonal edge of one muslin B (Diagram 2). Repeat to make 22 sets. Stitch one of each set together (Diagram 3).

2. Construct 22 rose blocks. Using green print Ds and muslin Bs, make 44 additional leaf sets (Diagram 2).

Stitch four muslin Ds to one rose C (Diagram 4). Then stitch one leaf set to opposite edges of block (Diagram 5). Repeat to make 22 rose blocks.

3. Piece center section. To make Row 1, stitch together one muslin E, one rose block on end, one muslin F, a second rose block on end, and a second muslin E (Diagram 6). Repeat to make Rows 3 and 5.

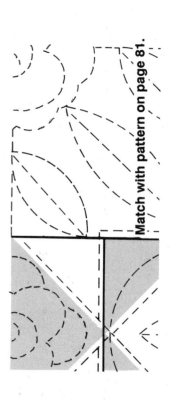

Match with pattern on page 81.

To make Rows 2 and 4, stitch together one rosebud block, one rose block and a second rosebud block. (The "bud" of the rosebud block is on the outside edges (Diagram 6).) Set aside extra blocks.

Stitch one $2^1/2$" x $16^1/2$" strip to each long edge of pieced section. Then stitch one $3^1/2$" x $16^1/2$" strip to top and bottom edges (Diagram 7).

4. Construct border strips. For one horizontal border strip, stitch together three rose blocks with two muslin As in a row (Diagram 8). Then stitch three muslin Es with two rosebud blocks in a row (Diagram 8). Stitch two rows together. Repeat for second horizontal border.

For one vertical border strip, stitch together two rosebud blocks, five muslin As and four rose blocks in a row (Diagram 9). Then stitch two muslin As, five rosebud blocks and four muslin Es in a row (Diagram 9). Stitch two rows together. Repeat for second vertical border.

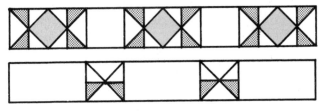

Diagram 8

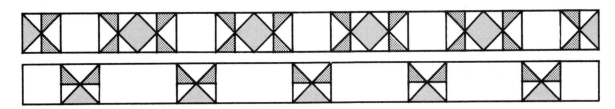

Diagram 9

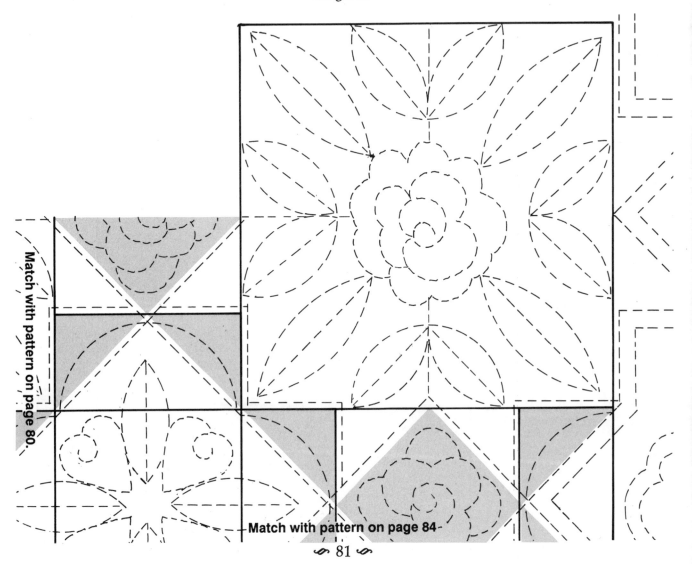

Match with pattern on page 80.

Match with pattern on page 84

✺ 81 ✺

5. Add border strips. Stitch pieced horizontal border strips to top and bottom of center section, placing rose-bud blocks on outside edge. Stitch pieced vertical border strips to each side of center section with rosebud blocks on outside.

Stitch $1^1/2$" x $26^1/2$" border strips to top and bottom edges. Then stitch $1^1/2$" x $33^1/2$" border strips to sides. Miter the corners.

6. Mark quilting lines. Trace quilting pattern onto quilt top.

7. Layer quilt. Place the quilt backing wrong side up. Center the fleece and quilt top. Baste.

8. Complete quilt. Quilt all marked lines with rose thread. Trim backing and fleece to match; quilt top. Bind the edge with rose bias.

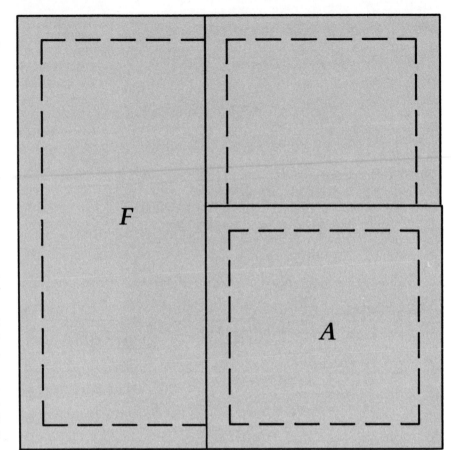

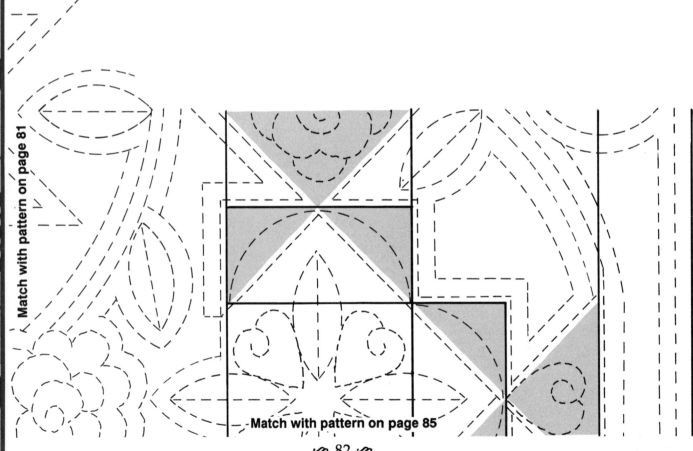

Match with pattern on page 81

Match with pattern on page 85

C

B

D

Match with pattern on page 80

Match with pattern on page 84.

Quilt Schematic ✌ 83 ✌

Match with pattern on page 81

Match with pattern on page 83.

Match with pattern on page 85.

Match with pattern on page 82

Match with pattern on page 84.

BASKET LID:

1. Construct basket top. Stitch one green print D and one muslin D together on one short edge (Diagram 1). Repeat to make eight sets. Stitch long edge of muslin D to one edge of rose C. Repeat on second edge of rose C (Diagram 2). Stitch one pieced triangle to each edge of muslin F (Diagram 3).

2. Mark quilting lines. Trace basket quilting pattern onto basket top; see page 81.

3. Layer quilt. Center the fleece and basket top. Baste.

4. Quilt. Quilt all marked lines with rose thread. Trim fleece to match basket top.

5. Make corded piping. Make 27" of corded piping from rose bias strips. Stitch piping to right side of basket top, rounding corners to correspond with box.

6. Complete basket. Using hot glue gun, place lace around basket lid, matching straight edge of lace with top edge of lid. Glue quilted basket top to lid.

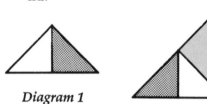

Diagram 1

Diagram 2

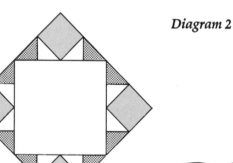

Diagram 3

PIN CUSHION:

Two 4" x 4" pieces of muslin fabric for quilt top and backing
Scraps of rose fabric
Scraps of green print fabric
One 4" x 4" piece of fleece
16" of small cording
16" of 1"-wide ecru gathered lace trim
Rose thread for quilting
Rose and green embroidery floss
Small amount of polyester stuffing
Small amount of potpourri (optional)

1. Cut four Pattern As and one 4" x 4" backing piece from rose fabric. Cut four Pattern Bs from green print fabric. Cut 1"-wide bias strips from rose fabric, piecing as needed, to equal 16". Make 16" of corded piping.

2. Fold one 4" x 4" muslin piece into quarters. Mark folds. Then mark diagonal lines from corner to corner. Using lines as guides, place rose As and green print Bs (Diagram 4). Applique.

3. Place the pincushion backing wrong side up. Center the fleece and pincushion top. Baste.

4. Quilt with rose thread around each leaf and heart piece. Then echo quilt 1/4" from outside edges of appliqued pieces. With embroidery floss, make bullion knot rosebud in center.

5. Stitch piping on right side of block matching raw edges. Stitch lace on piping, matching gathered edge of lace with raw edge of piping.

6. Stitch 4" x 4" rose piece to quilted top piece with right sides together leaving a small opening. Turn. Stuff with polyester stuffing and potpourri, if desired. Slipstitch opening closed.

Pattern A

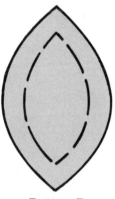

Pattern B

Diagram 4

STOCKING:

Fabrics needed: | **Cut sizes:**

Lavender: ¹/2 yard | Three of Template B
Two Stocking Patterns
One 1¹/2" x 4" piece for tab

Pink: scraps | Six of Template C

Mauve: ¹/2 yard | Six of Template C
Two stockings for lining

Tan/ rose print: scraps | Eight of Template A

Fleece: ¹/2 yard | Two stocking pieces

Also needed:

1¹/2 yards of ⁵/8"-wide rose double-faced satin ribbon
22 4-mm gold beads

TREE SKIRT:

Finished size: 60" across

Fabrics needed: | **Cut sizes:**

Pink: 1¹/2 yards | Eleven 2" x 44" strips

Mauve: 2³/4 yards | Eleven 2" x 44" strips
8¹/2 yards of 2"-wide bias for binding

Lavender: 5¹/2 yards | Twelve of tree skirt panel

Polyester fleece: 3³/4 yards | Eight of tree skirt panel

Also needed:

Mauve thread
6 yards of 5/8"-wide mauve double-faced satin ribbon
Approximately 200 4-mm gold beads

Christmas Without Snow

*It's good that there is Christmas
For the world
is much different then—
There's joy in the air,
Good will everywhere,
And hope in the hearts of men*

Thomas Malloy

PATCHWORK RABBIT:

Finished size: 9" x 9"

Fabrics needed: | **Cut sizes:**

Pink: ¹/4 yard | 2"-wide strips to equal 50"

Mauve: ¹/2 yard | 2"-wide strips to equal 50"
One Rabbit Pattern

Also needed:

Mauve thread
Stuffing
¹/4 yard of ⁵/8"-wide mauve double-faced satin ribbon
Two 4-mm gold beads

STOCKING:

1. Piece front. Stitch together one print A, one mauve B and second print A (Diagram 1). Repeat to make three strips. Stitch section together, adding two single print As (Diagram 2). Stitch together pink and rose C pieces, alternating colors, to make two strips of six blocks. Stitch one row to the top edge and one row to the bottom edge of the strips, aligning seams to points of diamonds (Diagram 3). Trim outside edges of diamond section even with checkerboard. Stitch pieced section to top of stocking front.

2. Construct stocking. Pin fleece to wrong sides of stocking front and back. Stitch stocking front and back with right sides together. Trim fleece from seam allowances. Turn. Stitch stocking lining pieces with right sides together, leaving an opening in seam above heel. Slide lining over stocking, placing right sides together and matching side seams. Stitch top edges. Turn through opening. Slip-stitch opening closed. Fold lining inside stocking. Fold 1¹/2" x 4" tab to measure ³/4" x 4". Stitch long edge. Trim to ¹/8" seam allowance. Turn. Fold to measure ¹/4" x 2". With raw ends together, place inside upper right corner. Tack.

3. Add bow. Cut one 52" length of ribbon. Tie into loose, 8"-wide bow. Tack to stocking. Sew beads to bow and to ribbon ends, placing ribbon toward toe of stocking (see photo).

PATCHWORK RABBIT:

1. Piece checkerboard. Sew together one long edge of 2"-wide strips of pink and mauve fabrics. Cut into 2"-wide segments. Sew segments together to make checkerboard of seven blocks wide by seven blocks long. Cut one Rabbit Pattern from checkerboard.

2. Construct rabbit. Stitch together right sides of checkerboard and mauve rabbit pieces, leaving opening on bottom edge. Clip curved seam allowances. Turn. Stuff firmly. Slipstitch opening closed.

3. Embellish rabbit. Tie ribbon in bow around rabbit's neck. Secure ribbon ends or checkerboard side with a bead near end.

Diagram 1

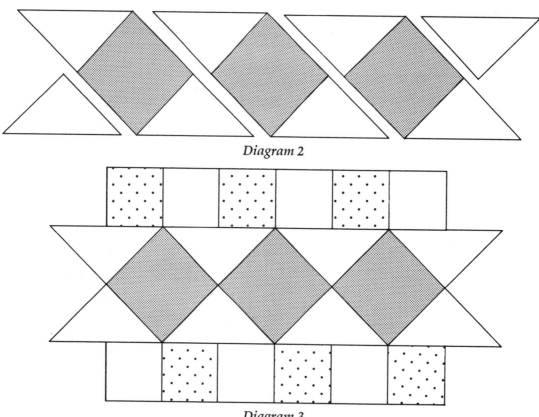

Diagram 2

Diagram 3

TREE SKIRT:

1. **Piece checkerboard.** Sew together one long edge of 2"-wide strips of pink and mauve fabrics. Cut into 2"-wide segments. Sew segments together to make checkerboard of 24 blocks wide by 38 blocks long. (Working with four strips of alternating colors makes the work go more quickly, but more strips than that may become awkward.) Cut four tree skirt pieces from the checkerboard fabric (Diagram 4).

2. **Construct tree skirt.** Pin one fleece piece to wrong side of four checkerboard tree skirt pieces and four lavender tree skirt pieces. Stitch together tree skirt, alternating pieces. Trim fleece from seam allowances. Stitch together eight lavender tree skirt pieces for lining. Pin tree skirt front to back with wrong sides together. Baste. Bind the center back, around outside edge and the second side of center back with pink bias. Begin binding neck of tree skirt by leaving a 24" tail for tie on bias, then bind neck, leaving second 24" tail.

3. **Embellish tree skirt.** Cut one 52" length of ribbon. Tie into loose, 8"-wide bow. Tack to tree skirt. Sew beads to bow and to ribbon ends (see photo for placement). Repeat for remaining lavender panels.

4. **Quilt tree skirt.** Stitch by machine through all layers on each seam between panels.

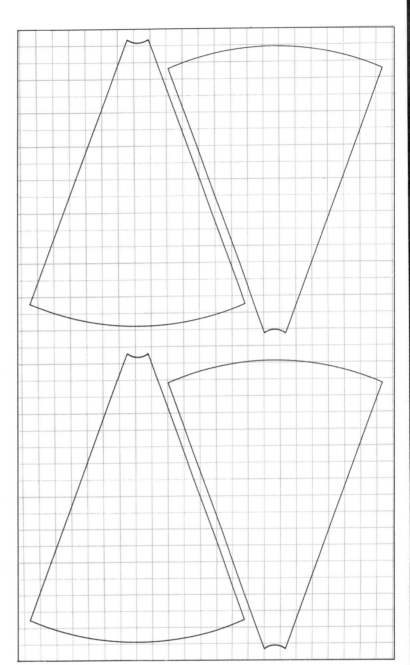
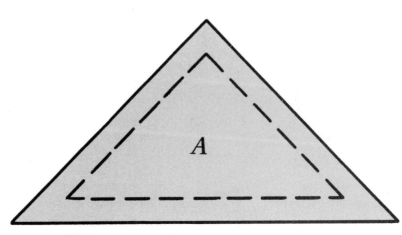

Diagram 4

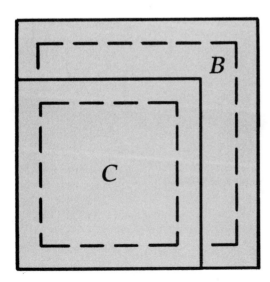

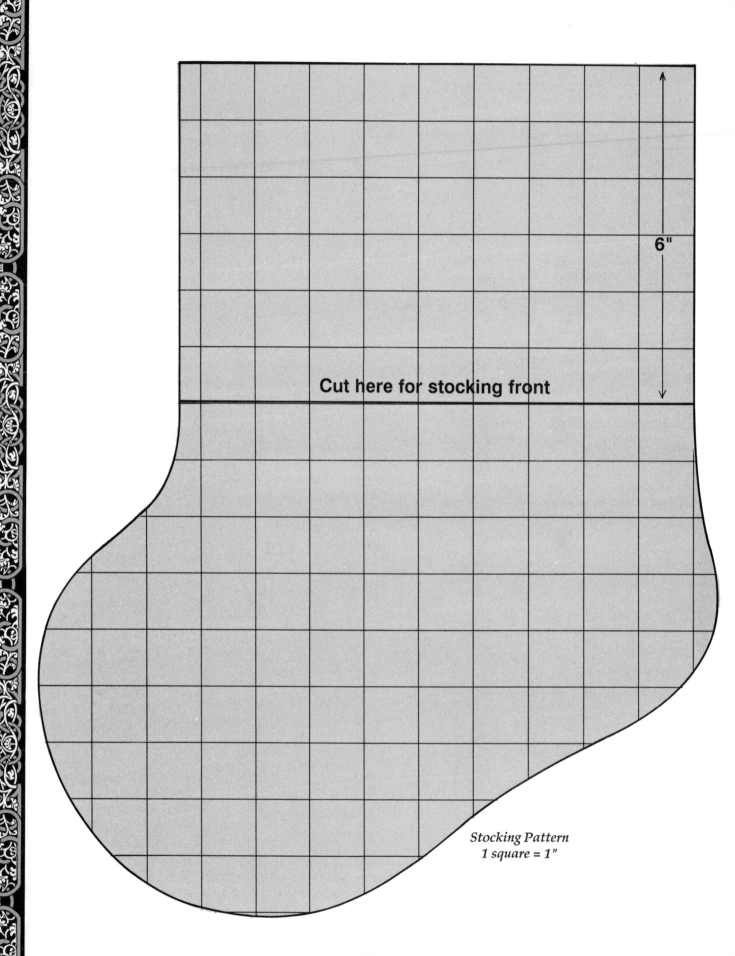

6"

Cut here for stocking front

Stocking Pattern
1 square = 1"

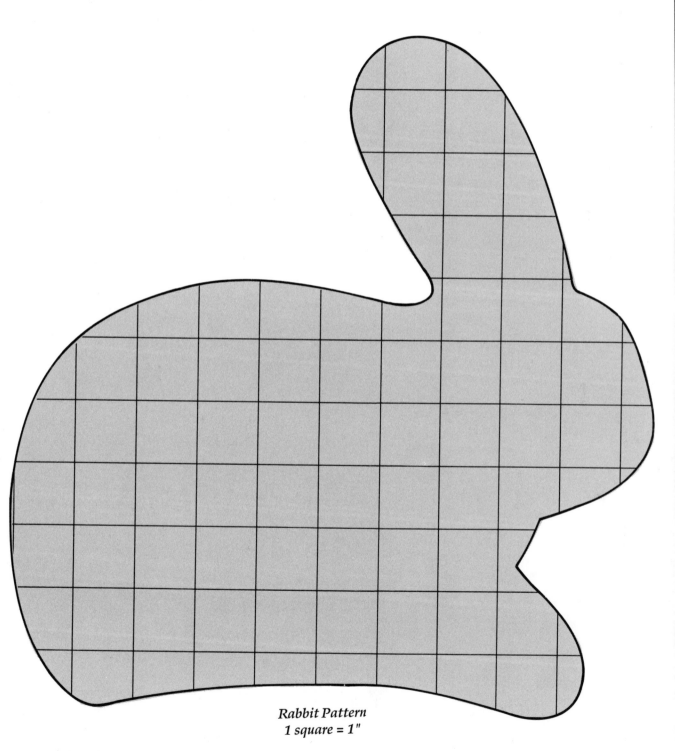

Rabbit Pattern
1 square = 1"

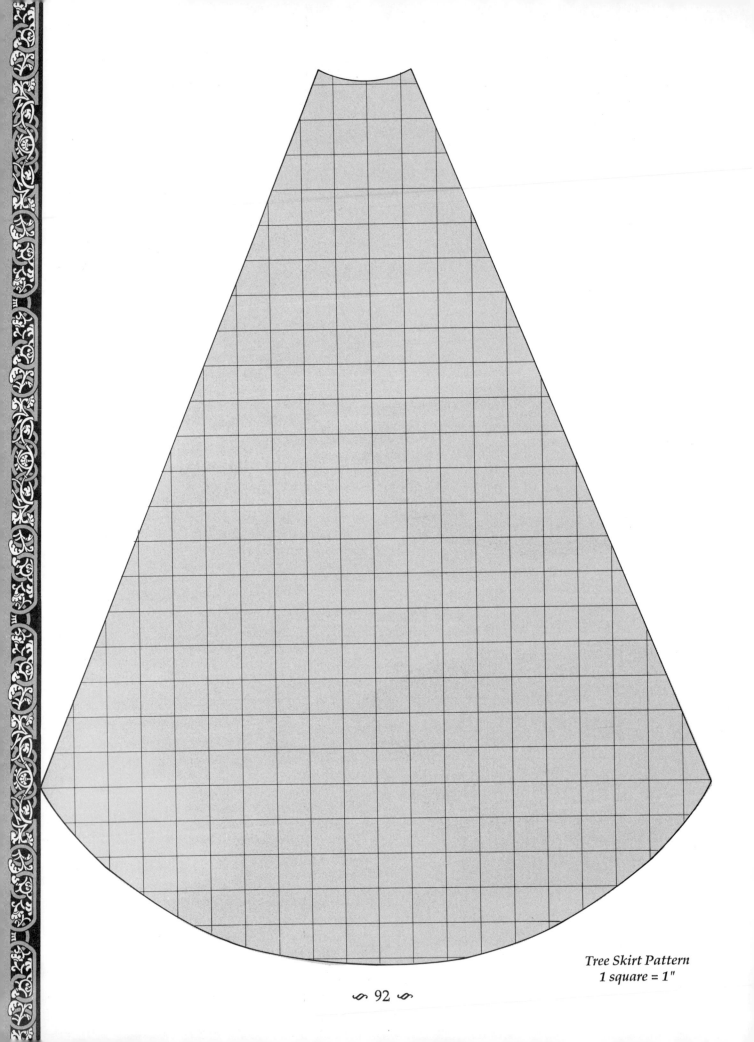

Tree Skirt Pattern
1 square = 1"

GENERAL INSTRUCTIONS

WHAT YOU WILL NEED

You will need the following equipment for some or all of the projects in this book:

✓ Dressmakers' pen or chalk or a #2 lead pencil for marking fabrics

✓ Clear quilters' ruler (some have 45-degree angles marked on them)

✓ Dressmakers' scissors (which are used for no purpose except cutting fabric)

✓ Rotary cutter and mat

✓ Embroidery and quilting needles

BEFORE YOU BEGIN

Before you start your first project—and because all quilt books are different—let us explain some of the principles used in *Victorian Quilting*.

◆ Templates include ¹/4" seam allowances. The seam allowance is also included in all measurements for pieces or strips (exceptions occur in "Patchwork Pair," "Perfect Pearls" and "Heirloom Treasures").

◆ Measurements for backing pieces and border strips are deliberately several inches larger than the finished size. This allows for some inevitable shifting between layers.

◆ Fabric requirements are based upon 44"/45"-wide selections. Wash, dry and press the fabrics. They will probably shrink, each a different amount. Trim the selvage; do not use selvages in any of the pieces.

◆ Each fabric is identified to match those used in the model in the photograph. That information is intended as a guide to you but should not confine you. Experiment with your own colors and textures, likes and dislikes.

◆ The finished size of a project is based upon measurements before any quilting is done.

MAKING TEMPLATES

Now you are ready to make your templates (patterns) and to cut the fabric. Use vinyl, cardboard, plastic or sandpaper for your templates, depending upon the size of each and the number you will need. Label each template.

CUTTING

Trace all of the pieces called for onto the wrong side of the fabric before cutting, beginning with largest pieces first. Also note the grain line of the fabric. Generally, one or more of the straight sides of the template will follow the grain line. Then cut all of the pieces for a project before you begin sewing. Identify each and store them in boxes or envelopes, anything that will keep an unruly piece in its place! Use a quilters' ruler to cut bias and border pieces.

Trace applique patterns without the seam allowances onto the right side of the fabric, using dressmakers' pen or pencil on light fabrics or dressmakers' chalk on dark fabrics.

PIECING QUILT TOP

Ready to start sewing? Of course, each quilt is made differently but, in general, here are some helpful ideas.

To piece the quilt by hand, which is a good choice for a design which has small pieces, it is necessary to work from precisely marked seam lines. Mark the seam lines on the wrong side of the fabric, leaving enough space between pieces for the ¹/4" seam allowances. Place the pieces with right sides together and sew the seams through the pencil lines. Join the pieces with a short running stitch using one strand of thread and a short needle. Begin and end each seam at seam line (not the edge of the fabric) with two or three backstitches.

With a machine-pieced work, the cutting line should be precise because the edge of the fabric can be aligned with the presser foot if it is ¹/4" wide. Sew all seams through to the cut edge unless you are inserting a piece at an angle.

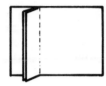

Press all seams to one side, usually toward the darker fabrics. Blocks should be square and each measure the same size. If problems occur with individual blocks, remove a few stitches and repair. Iron all parts—blocks, sashing and borders—before completing assembly.

Many quilts are constructed in rows. Sew blocks together to create rows, adding sashing if called for. Then sew rows together to complete the quilt top.

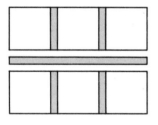

When setting blocks and rows together, avoid stretching them as you sew.

APPLIQUE

Appliques add detail and curved lines that are not available in pieced designs. In most cases, the seam allowances will be turned under, but if the appliqued pieces overlap, leave the seam allowances flat. Clip the seam allowances of inside curved edges. Cut out smaller, "V"-shaped pieces on outside corners to reduce bulk.

Fold the seam allowances to the wrong side. Pressing and/or basting is helpful. Place the design piece right side up on the right side of the fabric and slipstitch with close, small stitches using matching threads. Sometimes a decoration stitch is added to the edge.

BORDERS

Borders "frame" the quilt. The simplest borders are strips that are first pinned to two opposite edges. Then two more strips are joined to the remaining sides and extend beyond the ends of the first two strips.

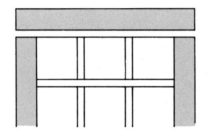

Mitered borders have diagonal seams in each corner.

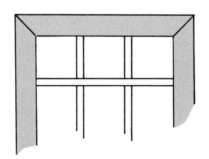

Center the border strip on each side. Pin, baste and sew strips to—but not through—seam line, and backstitch at each end. Repeat the process on all four sides. Your stitching lines should meet exactly at each corner. Fold

two adjacent border pieces together at corner. Mark, then sew a 45-degree angle. Trim ends to ¹/4" seam allowance.

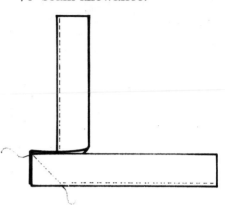

When your quilt border has more than one parallel strip of fabric, regardless of the width, it is probably easier to join all the strips together and miter them all at once.

LAYERING

Layer your quilt pieces and baste.

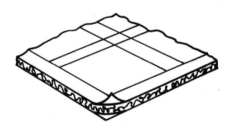

Begin basting, securing the layers together with safety pins. For small, lightweight pieces, safety pins are all you will need. For larger, bulkier projects, sew a loose running stitch from the center out, first dividing the quilt into quarters, then eighths.

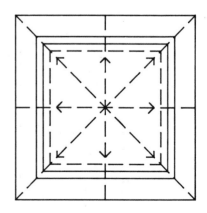

QUILTING

Quilting can turn even an ordinary quilt into a masterpiece. In addition to its beauty, quilting strengthens the piece.

To hand quilt, you will need thread and a small needle—a #9, #10 or #12. Quilting thread is waxed and is stronger than sewing thread, but it can be used, especially if you need a special color. Begin quilting in the center of the quilt. To bury your knot, insert the needle in the back and bring it out on the top. Then tug at the thread while the knot pops through the fabric and lodge it in the batting. Begin quilting with a very short backstitch. Quilt through all layers with small, even running stitches, using a thimble.

To fasten off, take a small backstitch on top of the quilt, bringing the needle through the loop that is formed. Tighten the thread to create a knot. Stitch your needle in the same hole as the knot, going into the batting, and tug enough to pop the knot under the fabric. Come to the top about 1" away, and take another very small backstitch. Come up $1/4$" away and cut the thread.

BINDING

Once the quilting is complete, trim the backing and batting to match the quilt top. A bias binding is the most common way to cover the raw edges. For a wallhanging or small piece that will not receive much wear, a single-layer bias binding is adequate. Stitch the right side of the binding and the quilt top together, matching raw edges. Fold the binding to the wrong side of the quilt, covering the raw edge and folding under $1/4$" seam allowance. Slipstitch folded edge to quilt back.

For a bed quilt or piece that needs a stronger binding, a double-layer bias binding is best. Cut the bias twice as wide as the single binding minus $1/2$". Fold the binding in half lengthwise; press. Matching all raw edges, stitch the binding and quilt top with right sides together. Fold the binding over the raw edge of the quilt and slipstitch the folded edge to the backing.

To miter corners of a bias binding, stitch the binding to the quilt top, stopping $1/4$" from the corner; backstitch.

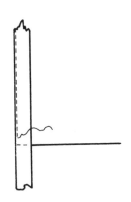

Fold the bias at the corner at a right angle. Resume stitching with a backstitch $1/4$" from the corner.

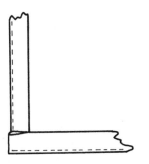

Then, when slipstitching the binding to the back, fold the bias with a mitered corner on both sides.

DON'T FORGET!

Be sure to sign and date your work! It enriches the piece for future generations. One way is to write your name and date on a scrap of washed fabric and slipstitch it to the back of the quilt. Another is to embroider the information onto muslin. If you have had experience cross-stitching, you might cross-stitch or backstitch your name and date on Aida 18 or a similar fabric.

GLOSSARY

APPLIQUE: A design made by cutting shapes of one or more fabrics and applying them by hand or machine to another surface (see General Instructions).

BACKING: The fabric which forms the bottom or back layer of the quilt.

BACKSTITCH: Very short stitches used in hand piecing at the beginning or end of a line of stitching to secure threads.

BASTING STITCHES: Temporary stitches used to hold fabric in place while quilting.

BATTING (sometimes called a batt): The filler or middle part that goes between the quilt top and the backing. It provides thickness and warmth to the quilt. Most batting is a polyester product and should be bonded. Some projects use cotton flannel.

BIAS: The diagonal of a woven fabric in which a true 45-degree angle is formed. The bias has the greatest amount of stretch.

BINDING: A narrow strip of fabric used to enclose the raw edges of the quilt top, batting and backing. It can be cut on either the straight grain or the bias. (See General Instructions for ways to attach bias).

BLOCK: A unit of patchwork, usually in the form of a square, repeated to construct an entire quilt top.

BORDER: Plain, pieced or appliqued band(s) of fabric surrounding the central section of the quilt top. (See General Instructions for ways to attach borders.)

CRAZY PATCH: A form of patchwork in which odd shapes of fabric are stitched to a foundation block. Embroidery stitches may accent seams.

ECHO QUILT: To quilt in concentric rows parallel to a seam or the edge of an appliqued piece.

"FUDGE": An irresistible chocolate candy, but in sewing, it means to hedge or cheat a little with fabric!

GRAIN: The lengthwise and crosswise threads of a woven fabric used in its construction.

GRID: Squares of uniform size such as those used in quilting patterns.

HAND QUILTING: Small running stitches which hold the three layers of the quilt together, either following a design which has been marked on the quilt top or following the outline of a pieced or appliqued block.

LAYERING: The process of placing the three layers of the quilt together.

LOFT: The springiness, or fluffiness, of a fiber.

MITER: Vertical and horizontal strips of fabric are joined at 45-degree angles, forming a 90-degree corner. Mitered corners are commonly used in constructing borders (see "Borders" in General Instructions).

PATTERN: Any design of a quilt usually repeated several times on the quilt top. Sometimes referred to as "design."

PIECING / PIECED BLOCK: Pieces of cut cloth sewn together to produce a pattern, usually in the form of a block.

QUILT TOP: The top layer of the quilt. It can be pieced, appliqued or a combination of the two.

QUILTING / QUILTING STITCHES: Stitches used to secure the three layers of the quilt together. The quilting can be done by either hand or machine.

RUNNING STITCH: A short, even stitch used for hand piecing.

SASHING: The strip of fabric used between blocks to separate and set them together.

SEAM ALLOWANCE: The distance between the cut edge of the fabrics and the stitching line.

SEAM: The stitched junction of two pieces of fabric, right sides together, with a 1/4" seam allowance. Can be done by either hand or machine.

SELVAGE: A small, almost invisible stitch used to secure a folded edge to a flat surface.

TEMPLATE: An individual model of a part of a pattern block made from cardboard, plastic, sandpaper or vinyl.